Samuel H. Sloan
Administrator of Estate
of K. Michael Goodall
with Will Annexed
461 Peachstone Terrace
San Rafael CA 94903
(415) 419-5980
917-659-3397
samhsloan@gmail.com

AF876152

IN THE SUPREME COURT OF THE STATE OF CALIFORNIA
No. S208895
After a Decision of the Court of Appeal
First Appellate District, Division Four
COURT OF APPEAL No. A137190
San Francisco Superior Court No. PTR-99-273030

BANK OF AMERICA N. A.,

Plaintiff and Respondent,

v.

SAMUEL H. SLOAN,

Objector and Appellant.

Goodall Estate Petition for Review Case No. S208895
California Supreme Court

Petitioner appeals herein from an order which denied a motion for Discovery. Please Note: The motion that Petitioner, who is the Administrator of the Estate of Michael Goodall with Will Annexed, filed on May 25, 2012 was NOT a motion for a rehearing of the May 16, 2012 order for the reason that petitioner believed and still believes that the May 16, 2012 was an interlocutory and therefore probably not appealable, since it did not finally decide the action. In addition, it could not be a motion for a rehearing because there was no hearing in the superior court. There was no sworn testimony, no declarations, no verifications, no evidence presented (because counsel for Bank of America said that the evidence had been lost). Thus, there was none of the things that normally accompany a judicial determination of facts.

The motion which Petitioner-appellant filed was entitled "MOTION TO COMPEL PRODUCTION OF DOCUMENTS AND FURTHER DESPOSITION AND DECLARATION OF SLOAN IN SUPPORT THEREOF."

The Grounds for this review are to secure uniformity of decisions from around the state because this case is running in parallel in two different courts and these two courts have reached the opposite decisions. They know about each other and refuse to change their rulings so review by an appellate court is necessary.

This case is running in parallel between two different courts in Marin and San Francisco, with opposite results. In the San Francisco case, the case is Case No. PTR 99-273030. In Marin County, the Case numbers are PRO1100596 and CV1204541.

A motion for discovery under the circumstances of this case is or should be appealable precisely because there has never been any discovery in this case except for a deposition of James R. Hastings in which he testified that he could not remember anything about this case and had lost or misplaced all his files of this case and so he had nothing to produce.

However, it was the Superior Court Judge and the Opponents who said that this was a motion for reconsideration. This is one of four appeals filed in the California Court of Appeal, all from the same case. The first two appeals, A137189 and A137190, were summarily dismissed and Petitions for Review are being filed in this court. The Remaining two appeals are A137739 and A137740. Those two appeals are still pending.

Review is necessary and appropriate by this court because this case is running in parallel between two different courts in Marin and San Francisco, with opposite results. In the San Francisco case, the case is Case No. PTR 99-273030. In Marin County, the Case numbers are PRO1100596 and CV1204541.

In almost every instance, the issues in the San Francisco Case are exactly the same as the issues in the Marin Case, yet the results have been the opposite. For example, the Bank of America filed a Statute of Limitations Claim in the Marin case. Judge Verna Adams dismissed that claim in a reasoned and lengthy opinion on April 16, 2012. Undaunted, Bank of America filed exactly the same claim in San Francisco, which resulted in an order from which an appeal is taken here.

Similarly, The Bank of America took the ruling by the San Francisco Court here and tried to enforce it over in Marin in a motion for summary judgment. However, the Marin County Superior Court Judge denied the claim by Bank of America, saying that the San Francisco order was interlocutory and non-final and thus non-enforcable in Marin. The Marin County judge ruled that Bank of America must file a claim to quiet title in Marin since the property is in Marin. However, throughout the two years that this litigation has been going on, Bank of America has been unwilling to submit its claims to the jurisdiction of the Marin courts, for reasons best known to Bank of America. This has resulted in this stalemate which will take action by the appellate courts to resolve.

Because of these conflicting decisions by different judges in different courts, the situation is in stalemate. The Goodall Estate consists of an estimated two million dollars in cash and securities plus a house known as "The Goodall Mansion" located at 461 Peachstone Terrace, San Rafael California 94903. Bank of America has the money, having stolen it back in 1999 which resulted in this case, PTR 99-273030, whereas the Estate of Goodall has possession and control of the house. Bank of America has been unsuccessful in its efforts to oust the Goodall Estate from the house.

There is nothing going on in the Superior Court Cases in either Marin or San Francisco at the present time. Only these four appeals are pending in the San Francisco case. Thus, it appears that unless this court reviews this case, the parties will be locked in stalemate for an extended period of time, possibly even for years or forever.

In order for this court to conclude that this was a motion for reconsideration and therefore non-appealable even though the motion says that it is a motion for discovery, this court must conclude that the prior order dated May 16, 2012 was a judgment. However, that order clearly was NOT a judgment. It did not use the word "judgment". It did not finally decide the action. It left unopened and undecided almost every question about this case.

Indeed, the Bank of America moved to enforce this order over in Marin County Superior Court and Judge Roy Chernus there said that the May 16 order was NOT a final judgment and was interlocutory.

On January 15, 2013, The California Court of Appeal dismissed summarily the appeal in this complicated case without waiting for the normal record, briefs and argument. Petitioner therefore did not get a chance to present his arguments to this court.

Since this court has never seen the record of this appeal because the Superior Court never had time to transmit it, it could not have understood the complex issues in this case. As Judge Roy Chernus of Marin County Superior Court stated in a one of the related cases in Marin County, "this is not your usual garden variety type of action" because while this case has been pending in the San Francisco Probate Court the same case has been pending over in the Marin County Probate Court. Two courts have been handling the same case.

Plaintiff here, Bank of America, lost their initial motions over in Marin County and then opted for the greener pastures in San Francisco Probate Court. As this case has progressed, every time Bank of America lost a motion over in Marin County they filed the same motion in San Francisco where they won.

Regarding the statute of limitations claim that Bank of America made in an "Additional Reply" in which the Administrator of the Goodall Estate did not have a chance to respond, Bank of America had made exactly the same Statute of Limitations claim in Marin County and Judge Verna Adams had dismissed that claim in a reasoned and lengthy opinion on April 16, 2012. Undaunted, Bank of America made that identical claim on San Francisco Probate Court.

Petitioner was prevented by the actions of opposing counsel and actions of the judge which made it impossible for him to file the appeal any sooner than he did. Indeed, Petitioner waited in the court room for the San Francisco Judge to sign his final order in this case so he could go down to the filing room to file this notice of appeal.

In view of the actions of the San Francisco Probate Judge in making this case "Appeal Proof" by among other things waiting a full two months before signing the order denying the petition for rehearing the judge prevented an earlier appeal. The order was submitted to the judge for signing on July 27, 2012. The judge did not sign it until September 26, 2012.

More than that, actions by Bank of America and Guide Dogs for the Blind unethically to chase Petitioner's Counsel off the case made it impossible for Petitioner to retain new counsel. They did this by repeatedly filing motions for sanctions against existing counsel. Their first motion for sanctions which demanded attorneys fees between $13,000 and $16,000 against both the Administrator of the Goodall Estate and his counsel was filed on June 29, 2012. That motion was denied by Judge Busch on June 19, 2012.

However, on the very next day, July 20, 2012, Bank of America filed a second motion for sanctions even though nothing had changed overnight since the first denial.

A Third Motion for Sanctions was filed by Bank of America on August 14, 2012.

All these motions for sanctions filed by a big and powerful Bank of America and their counsel one of the largest law firms in California had the effect of understandably frightening the counsel for the Goodall estate. As no man can serve two masters, Counsel for the Goodall estate felt that he had to withdraw as counsel for the estate in order to defend himself against these successive motion for sanctions which threatened his professional career.

Meanwhile, Sam Sloan, the Administrator of the Goodall Estate, the Petitioner here, found it impossible to retain another counsel because every other attorney is afraid of Bank of America and their attorney too. Nobody wants to stick their head in the lion's mouth.

As a result, Petitioner had no choice but to wait until these motions for sanctions and motion to withdraw were decided before he could file this notice of appeal. Petitioner was literally waiting in the courtroom for the judge to sign these orders so he could run down to the clerk's office and file this notice of appeal the same day.

If this court decides that this appeal is untimely in spite of these considerations, Petitioner requests that this appeal be construed as a writ petition. Since Petitioner does not have an appellate remedy since the court took so long to decide the motion, the time to appeal the underlying judgment had expired before he knew the outcome, but had petitioner appealed that judgment earlier, the trial court would then have lost jurisdiction to deal with the matter.

After considering this matter, this court should dismiss this case entirely. The proper Probate Proceeding involving the Goodall Estate is now pending over in Marin County Probate Court. Case No. PR 1100596. The Goodall wills are admitted into probate in Marin. Everything about this case happened over in Marin. The only reason Bank of America filed in San Francisco is they do not like the judge over in Marin.

In addition, Bank of America should not have been allowed to use the case number of this inactive case to file a new claim for a different cause of action. There was no activity in this case for

11 years from March 2000 to April 2011. This case should have been dismissed for inactivity under California Code of Civil Procedure Section 583.410. Thus this case should be dismissed with all orders vacated and Bank of America should be directed to file their claims in the right court, which is Marin County Probate Court.

We believe that the May 16, 2012 order is not a final judgment. It does not contain the word "Judgment". It does not include findings of fact and conclusions of law. It does not award money or property to anybody. It does not finally decide the action.

However, the orders of the San Francisco Court cannot be ignored because Bank of America claims that it is a judgment and they have moved to enforce it as a judgment.

In August and October, 2012 Bank of America filed two unlawful detainer actions in Marin County seeking to evict the Goodall heirs from the Goodall Mansion at 461 Peachstone Terrace San Rafael, California. These actions were unsuccessful, for the same reason Petitioner has stated from the beginning. Judge Chernus wrote:

> As against Sam Sloan and Kayo Kimura plaintiff seeks judgment for possession based on orders of the San Francisco Superior Court and the July 27, 2012, Sixty-day notice. Plaintiff has put its title to the property "at issue" in this unlawful detainer proceeding. The bulk of the allegations in the Complaint and the "Undisputed Facts" in support of the subject motion for summary judgment are addressed to plaintiffs extensive efforts by way of collateral proceedings in San Francisco Superior Court to confirm that the premises is an asset of the Trust for Michael created under the Goodall Trust dated September 12,1990, that title to the premises is in Bank America as trustee, and that plaintiff may administer the premises pursuant to the terms of Trust.
>
> Yet despite plaintiffs extensive allegations detailing the San Francisco proceedings, plaintiff does not actually allege or demonstrate via undisputed facts that the orders of the SF Sup. Court are final or that the issue of its title to the subject property has been fully and finally determined.
>
> Plaintiff appears to base its right to commence this unlawful detainer proceeding upon the Minute Order of the SF Superior Court dated July 19, 2012, denying defendant's petition for reconsideration as plaintiff

served the subject 60-Day Notice eight days later on July 27,2012, even though the court's order was not formally entered until September 27, 2012. (See Complaint, par. 19, and Exh. E) Even assuming the order denying defendant's petition for reconsideration constitutes a final and binding determination of plaintiffs title (though not specifically alleged) plaintiff served the 60-day notice before that order was formally entered on September 27, 2012. This unlawful detainer action was filed a mere 12-days later on October 9, 2012. As stated by the Court in Greenhut v. Wooden {1982} 129 Cal.App.3d 64,68, this is not your usual garden variety type of unlawful detainer action where the issue of title is strictly limited. Having put its own title in issue and by relying on the San Francisco Trust proceeding as the source of its authority to commence this proceeding plaintiff should demonstrate that title to the property has, in fact, been finally adjudicated in its favor. Plaintiff's pleading and evidence falls short of demonstrating a final adjudication of title in its favor and raises a question of fact whether the alleged 60-day notice was served prematurely.

As to defendants Hoppe and Thornally, a complaint for unlawful detainer must allege that the tenant continues in possession of the premises. (CCP $1161.) No cause of action for unlawful detainer exists if the tenant has quit before the action is filed. Defendants Hoppe and Thornally have filed answers admitting they have relinquished possession of the premises. In its motion, plaintiff claims that while Hoppe and Thornally have relinquished physical possession of the premises, "plaintiff is informed that Hoppe and Thornally have not relinquished their alleged right to possession of the premises." If a landlord wishes to determine rights to possession but not physical possession, it cannot do so by way of summary unlawful detainer; a quiet title action would be the proper remedy.

Thusly, Judge Chernus stated in essence the same thing petitioner Sloan has been saying from the first pleading which is that the only way for Bank of America to get what it wants is to file an action in Marin County. Bank of America can never succeed in obtaining access to real property in Marin by bringing a case in San Francisco.

This action by Bank of America should be dismissed and thrown out of court for a deeper reason, which is that Bank of America has never had standing in this case. Bank of America was never the legal trustee of the Goodall Trust. Kenneth and Rachel Goodall were the trustees. Upon the death of Kenneth, the Trust documents show that Michael became the co-trustee with his mother and upon her death Michael became the sole trustee. The documents showing this are annexed as exhibits here. At no time did Bank of America have any rights in this case. They simply usurped and stole this case because of the millions of dollars involved.

What happened is Bank of America stole the money, pure and simple. They have no right and no claim to the Goodall assets.

In addition, Guide Dogs for the Blind has no standing and no claim. The trust document upon which Bank of America and Guide Dogs for the Blind relies (although they have failed and refused to produce it and claimed to have lost it) does not establish their right.

Paragraph 6, note 1 of the petition filed by Bank of America contains the following noteworthy statement.

"The Provisions of the Bypass Trust are somewhat unclear with respect to the proper beneficiaries of the Trust for Michael in the wake of Mike Goodall's Death."

"Somewhat unclear" is a massive understatement or mis-statement. I have shown the trust documents to several attorneys specializing in such matters. All them say that the trust documents are nonsense. "Absurd", "ridiculous" and several other adjectives are used to describe these trust documents. A well known San Francisco attorney (who I prefer not to name) told me that the attorney who drew up this trust should be disbarred for incompetence.

On January 15, 2013, The California Court of Appeal dismissed summarily the appeal in this complicated case without waiting for the normal record, briefs and argument. Petitioner therefore did not get a chance to present his case to this court.

This is one of Four Appeals in just one of three cases Involving the Goodall Estate. Petitioner is the Administrator of the Estate of K. Michael Goodall with will annexed. This appointment came in a petition in probate filed in the Marin County Probate Court, Case No. PR 1100596.

Michael Goodall died on October 5, 2010 in his home known as "The Goodall Mansion" at 461 Peachstone Terrace in San Rafael, Marin County, California. Petitioner found the Goodall Will among his papers and filed it in Marin County Probate Court in January 2011.

On February 1, 2011, Petitioner filed a petition in probate. After consents were obtained from all of the heirs of the Goodall Estate, petitioner petitioned and after two hearings was appointed administrator of the estate.

Petitioner had the key to the house, as he has been a resident of the house. However, on February 28, 2011, while petitioner was away for a few days, there was a break-in and burglary in the house. The entire contents of the house was removed including all legal papers and documents of the Goodalls. When the burglary was discovered, 911 was called and this was reported as a burglary. Deputy Anthony Savas of the Marin County Sheriff's Department responded to the call. Deputy Savas said that he had been patrolling the area during the previous days and had observed a large trash dumpster in front of the house with a Spanish guy bringing stuff out of the house and putting it in the dumpster. However, Deputy Savas had not stopped to inquire, as this had seemed to be a routine case of somebody moving out.

After discovering that the Goodall Mansion had been burgled, the contents removed and the locks on the doors changed, Petitioner as well as heirs of the Goodall Estate searched for several weeks for the stolen Goodall stuff. Finally, by chance it was located in an Auction House in Alameda. The auction House identified Hamilton Kipp as the person who had brought the Goodall Estate stuff to the auction house. It was later established that Hamilton Kipp is an employee of Bank of America. Hamilton Kipp in turn had been told to break into the house and take all the stuff by James R. Hastings, a Marin County Estate Planning Attorney.

Petitioner filed an 850 Motion in Marin County Probate Court to recover estate property, namely the Goodall Stuff that had been taken by Hamilton Kipp. After two hearings before the Marin County Probate Judge, in June, 2011, Bank of America was forced to return the Goodall Stuff.

However, in the meantime, on April 21, 2011, Bank of America by way of collateral attack had filed a petition in San Francisco Superior Court seeking essentially to overturn the Marin County Probate Order which had listed among other things the Goodall Mansion as an asset of the Goodall Estate. In filing this new petition, Bank of America had used an old case number, PTR 99-273030. That was the number of a case Michael Goodall had filed in December 21, 1999 shortly after his mother had died in which he has sought the removal of Bank of America as Trustee on many grounds including the grounds that Bank of America was not the bank named in the Trust documents and that the proper trustee was Michael Goodall himself and if not himself then at least some bank not openly hostile to him as Bank of America was.

That 1999 case had never been finally decided because after a hearing Mike Goodall had run out of money to the fight the case and because Bank of America was using the funds in the Goodall Estate to fight him. The attorneys for Bank of America told him that if he did not stop fighting the case then the entire estate would be exhausted in attorneys fees and he would be left with nothing.

The attorneys for Bank of America have also been making the same statement in the current branch of the case, but this threat is less effective now because the Attorneys for Bank of America can and perhaps already have striped away all of the assets of the Goodall Estate, so there will be nothing left for the heirs anyway.

Only last week, an attorney for Bank of America informed one of the Goodall Heirs there is no money left in the estate. However, when Rachel Goodall died in June 1999 there was approximately one million dollars in the Goodall Estate plus the Goodall Mansion was worth an estimated $700,000. So, if truly the money is entirely gone that means that Bank of America has consumed the entire one million dollars in administration and attorneys fees. However, they must keep fighting this case because if they lose this appeal they will have to pay back the entire one million, plus interest.

The Living Trust set up by Kenneth and Rachel Goodall back in 1990 makes Michael Goodall the beneficiary of the trust. He also becomes the successor trustee of the trust if one or both of his parents dies. The only way a bank becomes a trustee is if Mike is declared incompetent by a court of competent jurisdiction. No such thing has happened.

The 1990 Trust names Security Pacific Bank as the Trustee. In a hearing on November 28, 2012 in Marin Superior Court, counsel for Bank of America said that Bank of America had become Trustee because:

> First, Security Specific Bank became Bank of America back in 1991. We were the successor. You'll probably take judicial notice of it, but that was a very big transaction.

See Transcript of the hearing of November 28, 2012 page 13 which is part of the record of this appeal.

However, this is not what happened. What happened was in 1992 Bank of America NT&SA purchased the assets of Security Pacific Bank. Then in 1998 Nations Bank in North Carolina purchased the assets of Bank of America NT&SA. Subsequently Nations Bank changed its name to Bank of America Corporation, which is a bank holding company located in Charlotte, North Carolina. Thus, the Bank of America today is a completely different entity from either Security Pacific Bank or Bank of America NT&SA. The operations headquarters of Bank of America is in Dallas Texas. It has no operations in California. This issue was raised by Mike Goodall's attorney, Rothman, when he filed this case back in 1999 pointing out that Bank of America today is not in any way the same bank as Bank of America back in 1990.

Counsel for Bank of America must be claiming that the two purchases of the assets of another bank in the 1992 and 1998 transactions also included the purchase of the "right" to be the successor Trustee to the Goodall Trust. It will take a review of the documents involved in these corporate transactions to determine if the purchase of the assets included the purchase of the right to be the successor trustee. However, none of this is of any moment because the January 1999 Amendment to the Goodall Trust, namely the Second Amendment to the Goodall Trust, makes Mike Goodall the co-trustee along with his mother. Thus, when Rachel Goodall died in June 1999 Michael Goodall survived as the sole trustee and Bank of America never became the legal trustee.

Bank of America knows this because an attorney for Bank of America drafted the Second Amendment to the Goodall trust.

Page 18 of a trust document, which Bank of America claims is controlling, but which we are prepared to prove was never signed by any of the Goodalls, contains the following provision:

> "(d) If MICHAEL does not survive the surviving settler and leaves no issue who survive the surviving settler, the trustee shall distribute the trust property twenty thousand dollars ($20,000) to each of the then living brothers and sisters of the trustor RACHEL A. Goodall and the remainder to GUIDE DOGS FOR THE BLIND OF MARIN, INC., of San Rafael California."

The problem is that this provision only applies if Michael dies BEFORE his parents do. However, Mike survived his parents by 11 years. Kenneth F. Goodall was born 01 Mar 1916 and died 10 Sep 1994 at age 78. His Social Security Number was 444-40-8884. Rachel A. Goodall was born 23 May 1916 and died 07 Jun 1999. Her Social Security Number was 359-07-1738. Kenneth Michael Goodall was born

13 Jan 1946 and died 05 Oct 2010. His Social Security Number was 559-70-3352.

Since Mike Goodall died 11 years after his parents did, that paragraph does not apply. More than that, nowhere in the entire documents, 40 pages long, is there any mention of what happens if Mike dies after his parents do, except that the trust documents state that the trust is "dissolved" after the death of Mike Goodall.

This provision and the entire document makes it completely 100% clear that the Goodall Estate belongs entirely to Mike Goodall and his heirs, unless Mike Goodall dies before his parents do. There is no possible way that Guide Dogs for the Blind gets anything out of the Goodall Estate. Under no interpretation of the Goodall Trust does Guide Dogs for the Blind get anything.

Yet, Bank of America, in its initial petition filed in San Francisco Superior Court, said that it was due to drafting errors that the trust documents mistakenly do not give any money to Guide Dogs for the Blind. Bank of America asked the Superior Court to in effect rewrite the trust documents so as to give the Goodall Estate to the Dogs.

At the first hearing in San Francisco Superior Court on May 25, 2011, Petitioner appeared *in pro per* because he felt it absurd and ridiculous that Bank of America would file their petition, because the trust documents clearly DO NOT give any part of the Goodall Estate to the Dogs and secondly because this case was already pending as a probate case in Marin County that clearly had jurisdiction. The Goodalls all lived and died in Marin County, all of their property including their house was in Marin County, all their documents were executed in Marin County and there was nothing about this case that had anything to do with San Francisco County. Thus, San Francisco County obviously does not have jurisdiction. Petitioner expected that the San Francisco Court would throw the case out immediately.

In addition, Guide Dogs for the Blind is behind all of the other heirs. The trust provides that each of the Goodall siblings gets $20,000. Rachel Goodall had five siblings, three brothers and two sisters, and Kenneth Goodall had two brothers. Many of them are dead but they all married and had children, some of whom were adopted. There are about twenty Goodall heirs listed on the service list and they all have the right to contest this case. Clearly, only the Marin County Probate Court has the jurisdiction, venue and competence to decide these claims.

In addition, the direct heirs of Michael Goodall may have a claim. The trust provides that his wife and/or children inherit from the trust.

Guide Dogs for the Blind are at the bottom of the totem pole. This case goes to the dogs and they get money only after all these other people and even then the Dogs do not get anything unless Michael dies before either of his parents do, which did not happen.

Because of all these factors, Petitioner did not take seriously the petition filed by Bank of America in San Francisco. Petitioner assumed that the San Francisco case would either be dismissed or else transferred to the right court, which was Marin County Probate Court.

Petitioner was thus shocked when the San Francisco judge with a wave of the hand and without giving any reason for the decision or indeed without saying anything at all ruled in favor of Bank of America and signed an order that had been handed up without even allowing the Petitioner to see and comment on the order that was being signed.

Petitioner then realized that he had better retain counsel. After a long search, Petitioner found a qualified attorney willing to represent the Goodall Estate on a Contingency Fee basis. This was necessary because Bank of America had already taken all the money. The Goodalls had never had an account with Bank of America, not even a simple checking account. Col. Goodall was retired military officer, so most of the Goodall money was with USAA Investment Management in San Antonio, Texas. There were also smaller amounts with mutual finds and stock trading accounts. None of this was with Bank of America or anywhere in the state of California.

Right after Rachel Goodall had died in June 1999, Bank of America through its attorney James R. Hastings had contacted USAA Investment Management and directed that all Goodall funds be transferred to Bank of America. Mike Goodall had not been told about this and had no idea that this had happened. In short order, all of the bank accounts that Mike Goodall had been operating were stripped of their assets. Mike Goodall was left destitute and without funds. That is the reason why he filed this case on December 21, 1999.

Bank of America completely stonewalled, as they continue to do this day. They refused and still continue to refuse to give Mike Goodall or indeed any of the Goodalls any accounting or any information about what happened to the Goodall Millions. It was as if the funds had disappeared into a Black Hole.

Just before Kenneth Goodall died in 1994 he had an accounting done of the funds. The accounting shows that the Goodalls had very slightly less than one million dollars in cash and securities plus the fully paid for house. Rachel Goodall was an excessively frugal person. She basically never spent money on anything, so the money should at least have doubled since 1994.

After the adverse ruling on May 25, 2011, Petitioner was able to retain counsel in time for the next hearing in San Francisco Probate Court. Meanwhile, several hearings on the same subject matter had been held in Marin County Probate Court.

It is important at all times to remember that this case is running in parallel in two different courts: San Francisco Superior Court and Marin County Probate Court. Obviously, the Marin County Court is the right court and at each hearing in San Francisco Petitioner has demanded transfer of this case to Marin.

At the next hearing in San Francisco, Bank of America brought attorney James R. Hastings to court prepared to have him testify as a witness as he had been attorney for both the Goodalls, the Goodall Trust and the Bank of America. Hastings was going to testify that the money should go to the Dogs. This was one of just many obvious conflicts on interest by James R. Hastings. However, Petitioner's new counsel Sam Ware asked for the opportunity of discovery. Bank of America protested vehemently and said that there should be no discovery at all. They especially objected to any discovery of the money. They refused to reveal anything about the Goodall millions, how much it was, were they had gotten it from and what they had done with it.

Finally, Judge Mary Wiss agreed that there should be some discovery. Whereas Bank of America wanted to hold a hearing and finish the case that day, the superior court judge said that there should be discovery.

However, as will be seen there has never been any discovery on this case, because Bank of America has been completely stonewalling. Not one document has been produced either by Bank of America or attorney James R. Hastings. Bank of America has absolutely refused to produce anything. James R. Hastings has testified that he has lost the files and thus does not have anything. In addition he has stated that to provide any discovery would violate the attorney

Client Privilege of Bank of America because he was counsel for Bank of America at the same time that he was counsel for the Goodalls.

Sam Ware then subpoenaed James R. Hastings for a deposition and required him to bring all documents and files pertaining to this case. Hastings appeared for the deposition on November 14, 2011 but did not bring any documents at all. His attorney Don Lesser said that the subpoena was overbroad and as Hastings had been attorney for Bank of America too it would violate the attorney client privilege of Bank of America and that the files and notes pertaining to this case had all been lost. At the oral deposition, Hastings testified that basically he could not remember anything about the case.

On December 14, 2011 Sam Ware filed a motion for discovery and production of documents pertaining to this case.

On December 29, 2011, Don A. Lesser, Counsel for James Hastings, filed opposition to the motions for discovery, saying that it would be "oppressive and burdensome" upon James R. Hastings and also violate the attorney client privilege of Bank of America because James R. Hastings had been attorney for Bank of America at the same time that he was attorney for the Goodall and the Goodall Trust.

Not long thereafter Don Lesser withdrew as counsel for James R. Hastings.

On January 20, 2012, Judge Busch denied the motion for production of documents, especially the trust Document, but said that James R. Hastings was required to search his files to look for the trust and if he could find it he was required to produce it and otherwise he must file a declaration stating what efforts he had made to find the trust.

On February 2, 2012, James R. Hastings filed a declaration stating that he had searched all his files and was unable to find the trust.

On February 6, 2012, Nancy Rodgers, a friend and neighbor of the Goodalls, filed a declaration stating that her purported signatures on the Goodall Wills, which were pour over wills pouring money into the trust, were not her signatures and she had never signed such a document. As there had never been any money in the trust, these pour over wills were essential to the claims by Bank of America and Guide Dogs for the Blind to be entitled to any of the Goodall millions.

After several more pleasings were filed on all sides, on April 24, 2012, Bank of America filed an additional reply asserting for the first time in this case that objections to the 1994 Trust were time-barred by a Statute of Limitations. Although this was the first time Bank of America had made this claim in this case, they had made exactly the same claim in the parallel proceeding going on in Marin County Probate Court. That claim had been dismissed by Marin County Probate Judge Verna Adams in a lengthy and reasoned decision on April 16, 2012. The statute of limitations claim was also entirely bogus for several reasons the most obvious being that Michael Goodall had indeed contested the right of Bank of America to be the trustee by filing this very case on December 21, 1999. Also, the statute of limitations claim was not accompanied by any evidence or a declaration in support. In addition, the words "as amended" had been omitted or when it was included, obviously it logically referred to the 1999 Amendment to the Trust which had made Mike Goodall the Trustee. The 1990 Trust had made Michael Goodall the beneficiary of the trust and the 1999 Amendment had made Michael the co-trustee of the trust, so there was no reason for Michael to object to either of them.

Because of the shortness of time before the previously scheduled hearing, Samuel Sloan and his counsel did not have time to respond to this "additional reply" and so asked for additional time which was denied from the bench. And so, Judge Busch signed the order dated May 16, 2012 from which the first appeal is taken, without a fact hearing of any kind and without any findings of fact or conclusions of law.

On May 25, 2012, seven days after the entry of the order of May 16, 2012, Samuel Sloan filed through counsel a motion for discovery to compel the production of documents including the documents forming the basis of the newly made statute of limitations claim. This was not filed as a motion for reconsideration, because Sloan through counsel deemed the May 16, 2012 order to be an interlocutory order, not a final judgment, because, among many other things it does not use the word "judgment", and does not dispose of all of the issues involved in this case. However, this motion was filed within the time limit for motions for reconsideration to be on the safe side in case the courts were later to decide that it was a judgment.

Sam Sloan, Administrator of the Goodall Estate, had been caught off guard by the May 16, 2012 decision because he had naturally assumed that there would be some sort of trial or fact hearing and Bank of America would be required to present their evidence if any before the court would rule. It was not to be expected that the judge would decide this complicated case abruptly from the bench without any hearing. Because of this surprise ruling, the administrator started searching through the 40 or 50 storage boxes of material Bank of America had stolen when they broke into the Goodall Mansion on February 28, 2011 but then were forced to return on June 10, 2011 by proceedings in the Marin County Probate Court.

During these searches, the administrator found a treasure trove of documents. All or almost all of these documents had been prepared by James R. Hastings, Attorney for Bank of America, so Bank of America had these documents all along but had failed to produce them. Of great importance was a Power of Attorney the Goodall Parents, Kenneth and Rachel Goodall, had given their son Michael on August 24, 1994 on the Death Bed of Kenneth, placing Michael with power of attorney over the Goodall Trust. This proved that the claim by the Attorney of Bank of America that the Goodall parents did not trust Michael with their money was false. Also included in the same treasure trove of documents was a signed health care directive by Kenneth Goodall that he be allowed to die of the Esophageal cancer of which he was suffering at the time and an unsigned 1994 Goodall Trust showing that Kenneth had never signed the 1994 amendment to the trust. Kenneth Goodall was in the final stages of cancer and a feeding tube had been inserted in his abdomen on July 17, 1994. He died on September 10, 1994. These documents were included in the exhibits Sloan filed in his May 25, 2012 motion.

On the same date, Sloan filed a declaration of David S. Moore, a highly regarded forensic document examiner, who stated that upon comparing the known and authentic signatures of Kenneth Goodall found on other documents, on checks, on his personal notebook and the like and comparing them with the signature on the purported 1994 amendment to the trust, they were not consistent but he could not made a final determination as to whether the signature was authentic or not without being allowed to examine the actual trust document, but such an examination had been denied.

On June 27, 2012, Gary Rothstein, attorney for Bank of America served on Sam Sloan and his counsel Sam Ware a motion for sanctions against the Motion for Discovery dated May 25, 2012 asking for sanctions against Sam Sloan personally and against Sam Ware personally in the amount of $16,000 for filing the motion for discovery which they deemed to be a motion for reconsideration. In a cover letter, Gary Rothstein, attorney for Bank of America, stated that unless the motion for reconsideration were withdrawn he would file the motion for sanctions, effectively blackmailing the Goodall Estate.

It is important to remember here that Sloan is a volunteer administrator of the trust because the Goodall Trust has no money because Bank of America stole it all and Sloan is not named in the will. In addition, Attorney Sam Ware took this case as a contingency case. By serving this motion for sanctions Bank of America was threatening Sloan and his counsel with a substantial financial loss whereas they had nothing to gain from this case.

So, the Administrator of the Goodall estate had everything to lose and nothing to gain by continuing this case.

On June 29, 2012 Guide Dogs for the Blind joined this motion by filing their own motion for sanctions for filing this petition for rehearing.

Nevertheless, the administrator and his counsel did not Cave in yet.

A hearing was held on these motions on July 19, 2012. Judge Busch denied the motion which he deemed to be a motion for reconsideration and he also denied the motion by Bank of America and Guide Dogs for the Blind for Sanctions against the Administrator of the Goodall Estate and Sam Ware, Counsel for the Goodall Estate.

On July 20, 2012, the very next day, Bank of America filed a new motion for Sanctions against the Administrator of the Goodall Estate and against Sam Ware Counsel for the Goodall Estate seeking sanctions in the amount of between $13,000 and $16,000 against each of them. This motion had been denied from the bench the previous day so obviously nothing had changed.

On July 27, 2012, the parties submitted for the judge's signature an order denying the motion for reconsideration heard on July 19, 2012. Sam Sloan, Administrator of the Estate, planned and intended to file a notice of appeal as soon as the order was signed. Instead the judge sat on the order for two full months and did not sign in until September 26, 2012. It was entered the following day. This delay of two months put it past the normal time for filing a notice of appeal.

On August 14, 2012, Bank of America filed a third Motion for Sanctions against the Administrator of the Goodall Estate and his attorney.

On September 7, 2012, as a result of having three successive motions for sanctions filed against him, Sam Ware filed a motion to be relieved as counsel. He said that he could not effectively oppose the repeated motions for sanctions against him while also acting as counsel for the estate. No man can serve to masters so he needed to be relieved as counsel so that he could defend himself against actions by Bank of America and their counsel which threatened his professional career.

Now again Sloan could not file his notice of appeal because he had to wait until the judge decided the motion for sanctions and the motion by his counsel to withdraw to escape the sanctions. As Sloan was represented by Counsel he could not file the Notice of Appeal by himself. In addition, as these motions affected the merits of the case and the judge was retaining jurisdiction over the case there remained the possibility that the judge would reverse himself and the case would continue.

Finally, the judge held his hearing on the motion to withdraw which was strenuously opposed by Sloan and granted the motion on November 15, 2012. On the same day, Judge Busch held his hearing on the motion for sanctions and denied that motion, basically saying that there was enough grounds for Counsel for the Goodall Estate to file a motion for reconsideration but not enough grounds for him to grant it.

On September 21, 2012, Judge Busch signed the order denying the Motion for Sanctions. Sloan filed his notice of appeal the very same day.

ARGUMENT

The Court of Appeal dismissed the first appeal as untimely. Petitioner contends that it was not untimely because of the inappropriate and indeed unethical actions of both opposing counsel and the Superior Court judge. Opposing counsel kept filing motions even after the order appealed from. They filed three successive motions for sanctions in the amount of more than $13,000 against Petitioner and his counsel. It is important that Petitioner is a unpaid volunteer administrator because there is no money in the Goodall Estate and trust as Bank of America stole all the money. Petitioner is also not an heir to the Goodall estate. However, the real heirs to the Goodall Estate are depending on Petitioner to win this case because if Bank of America wins the heirs will get nothing zero, as all the money will go to the Dogs.

So, by filing these groundless motions by two of the biggest law firms in San Francisco Petitioners counsel became afraid to file an appeal. In addition, Petitioner could not retain another attorney either as every attorney he consulted was afraid that he too would be on the wrong end of a motion for sanctions by Bank of America.

Next, Petitioner filed a motion for discovery. The superior court had ruled in favor of a new claim by Bank of America that a Statute of Limitations barred petitioner's defense. This claim was obviously bogus because Mike Goodall had filed this very case back in 1999 to object to Bank of America being the trustee.

Thirdly, the judge delayed two months in signing the order. This delay of two months by the judge was what put the case over the time limit to file the appeal.

The order was submitted to the judge for signing on July 27, 2012. The judge did not sign it until September 26, 2012.

Next the order that Judge Busch has not been after proper notice and a hearing. Indeed, there has never been a fact hearing in this case. There has never been sworn testimony of any witnesses. There has been no discovery. No documents have been produced. Hastings says that he has lost the trust documents. If you look at the case files you will see that there have been no declarations, no exhibits, no verifications, no findings of facts and conclusions of law.

Neither Bank of America nor Guide Dogs for the Blind have ever filed a brief or a memorandum of law in this case. They have never cited a single case, they have never explained upon what legal grounds or theory of law they are entitled to proceed. They have not even explained what they are even doing appearing in this case as the Goodalls all died more than two years ago. They have no standing to be appearing in this case. Only the contestants, namely Guide Dogs and the legitimate heirs have standing.

Meanwhile, James R. Hastings, who says that he has lost the documents, is teaching a class in Estate Planning. On page 15 of the current Tamalpais Union High School District Summer Camp Sneak Preview there is an ad for the next course by James Hastings. It is called Estate Planning 101. The next class starts on April 23, 2013 and the fee to attend the class is $25.

In The Alternative this Court Should Treat this as a Writ Petition

Petitioner has annexed a verification to satisfy one of the requirements for a writ petition. Under Olson v. Cory (1983) 35 Cal.3d 390, 401 [197 Cal. Rptr. 843, 673 P.2d 720] an appeal can only be considered as a writ petition under entirely unusual circumstances. It is submitted that the unusual circumstances exist here in that this case is running in parallel in two different courts and the courts have ruled in the opposite way. The Marin Courts have ruled in favor of Petitioner whereas the San Francisco court has ruled in favor of Bank of America.

At a hearing in Marin County Superior Court on November 28, 2012 in which Bank of America sought to enforce the order from which this appeal was taken, Judge Roy Chernus ruled that the May 2012 order was not a final judgment and was interlocutory. According to that ruling this appeal is unnecessary. However, Bank of America disagrees. They consider May 2012 the San Francisco order to be the final judgment. As a result this case is stalemated.

Of immediate concern is the court felt that the appeal from the May 16, 2012 was untimely. However, Petitioner contends that this is not correct because Petitioner was prevented by the actions of opposing counsel and actions of the judge which made it impossible for him to file the appeal any sooner than he did. Indeed, Petitioner waited in the court room for the San Francisco Judge to sign his final order in this case so he could go down to the filing room to file this notice of appeal.

In view of the actions of the San Francisco Probate Judge in making this case "Appeal Proof" by among other things waiting a full two months before signing the order denying the petition for rehearing the judge prevented an earlier appeal. The order was submitted to the judge for signing on July 27, 2012. The judge did not sign it until September 26, 2012.

More than that, actions by Bank of America and Guide Dogs for the Blind unethically made it impossible for Petitioner to retain new counsel. They did this by repeatedly filing motions for sanctions against existing counsel. Their first motion for sanctions which demanded attorneys fees between $13,000 and $16,000 against both the Administrator of the Goodall Estate and his counsel was filed on June 29, 2012. That motion was denied by Judge Busch on June 19, 2012.

However, on the very next day, July 20, 2012, Bank of America filed a second motion for sanctions even though nothing had changed overnight since the first denial.

A Third Motion for Sanctions was filed by Bank of America on August 14, 2012.

All these motions for sanctions filed by a big and powerful Bank of America and their counsel one of the largest law firms in California had the effect of understandably frightening the counsel for the Goodall estate. As no man can serve two masters, he felt that he had to withdraw as counsel for the estate in order to defend himself against these successive motion for sanctions which threatened his professional career.

Meanwhile, Sam Sloan, the Administrator of the Goodall Estate, the Petitioner here, found it impossible to retain another counsel because every other attorney is afraid of Bank of America and their attorney too. Nobody wants to stick their head in the lion's mouth.

As a result, Petitioner had no choice but to wait until these motions for sanctions and motion to withdraw were decided before he could file this notice of appeal. Petitioner was literally waiting in the courtroom for the judge to sign these orders so he could run down to the clerks office and file this notice of appeal the same day.

If this court decides that this appeal is untimely in spite of these considerations, Petitioner requests that this appeal be construed as a writ petition. Since Petitioner does not have an appellate remedy since the court took so long to decide the motion, the time to appeal the underlying judgment had expired before he knew the outcome, but had petitioner appealed that judgment earlier, the trial court would then have lost jurisdiction to deal with the matter.

If this court finds the appeal untimely, this court should considering the merits on a writ petition, on the ground that there was no appellate remedy. Petitioner in no way caused this delay.

After considering this matter, this court should dismiss this case entirely. The proper Probate Proceeding involving the Goodall Estate is now pending over in Marin County Probate Court. Case No. PR 1100596. Everything about this case happened over in Marin. The only reason Bank of America filed in San Francisco is they do not like the judge over in Marin.

We believe that the May 16, 2012 order is not a final judgment. It does not contain the word "Judgment". It does not include findings of fact and conclusions of law. It does not award money or property to anybody.

However, the orders of the San Francisco Court cannot be ignored because Bank of America claims that it is a judgment and they have moved to enforce it as a judgment.

This action by Bank of America should be dismissed and thrown out of court for a deeper reason, which is that Bank of America has never had standing in this case. Bank of America was never the legal trustee of the Goodall Trust. Kenneth and Rachel Goodall were the trustees. Upon the death of Kenneth, the Trust documents which are annexed as exhibits show that Michael became the co-trustee with his mother and upon her death Michael became the sole trustee. The documents showing this are annexed as exhibits here. At no time did Bank of America have any rights in this case. They simply usurped and stole this case because of the millions of dollars involved.

What happened is Bank of America stole the money, pure and simple. They have no right and no claim to the Goodall assets.

In addition, Guide Dogs for the Blind has no standing and no claim. The trust document upon which Bank of America and Guide Dogs for the Blind relies (although they have failed and refused to produce it and claimed to have lost it) does not establish their right.

Paragraph 6, note 1 of the petition filed by Bank of America contains the following noteworthy statement.

"The Provisions of the Bypass Trust are somewhat unclear with respect to the proper beneficiaries of the Trust for Michael in the wake of Mike Goodall's Death."

"Somewhat unclear" is a massive understatement or mis-statement. I have shown the trust documents to several attorneys specializing in such matters. All them say that the trust documents are nonsense. "Absurd", "ridiculous" and several other adjectives are used to describe these trust documents. A well known San Francisco attorney (who I prefer not to name) told me that the attorney who drew up this trust should be disbarred for incompetence.

For all of these reasons this appeal should be reinstated.

Dated :February 25, 2013

Respectfully Submitted,

Samuel H. Sloan
Administrator of Estate
of K. Michael Goodall
with Will Annexed
461 Peachstone Terrace
San Rafael CA 94903
(415) 419-5980
917-659-3397
samhsloan@gmail.com

IN THE SUPREME COURT OF THE STATE OF CALIFORNIA
No. S208895

BANK OF AMERICA N. A.,

Plaintiff and Respondent,

v.

SAMUEL H. SLOAN,

Objector and Appellant.

Verification:

Sam Sloan declares:

I have read the Petition for Review I filed in this matter, and I declare under penalty of perjury under the laws of the State of California and the contents thereof are true and correct to the best of my knowledge and belief.

DATED: February 25, 2013

Sam Sloan

COPY

ORIGINAL

IN THE COURT OF APPEAL OF THE STATE OF CALIFORNIA

FIRST APPELLATE DISTRICT

DIVISION FOUR

FILED

JAN 15 2013

Court of Appeal - First App. Dist.
DIANA HERBERT
By ______ DEPUTY

BANK OF AMERICA N.A., Plaintiff and Respondent, v. SAMUEL SLOAN, Objector and Appellant.	A137190 (San Francisco County Super. Ct. No. PTR99273030)

Appellant Samuel Sloan purports to appeal from a September 27, 2012 order denying his motion for reconsideration.

A court's ruling on a motion for reconsideration is not appealable. (Code Civ. Proc. § 1008, subd. (g).)

The appeal is dismissed.

Dated: JAN 15 2013

______ P.J.

COPY ORIGINAL

IN THE COURT OF APPEAL OF THE STATE OF CALIFORNIA

FIRST APPELLATE DISTRICT

DIVISION FOUR

FILED

FEB - 6 2013

Court of Appeal - First App. Dist.
DIANA HERBERT
By ________ DEPUTY

BANK OF AMERICA N.A., Plaintiff and Respondent, v. SAMUEL SLOAN, Objector and Appellant.	A137190 (San Francisco County Super. Ct. No. PTR99273030)

BY THE COURT:

Appellant's petition for rehearing, filed on January 29, 2013, is denied.

Dated: FEB - 6 2013

_______________ P.J.

SUPREME COURT OF THE STATE OF CALIFORNIA

PETITION FOR REVIEW

Exhibit A

Order of San Francisco Superior Court dated May 15, 2012

MANATT, PHELPS & PHILLIPS, LLP
GARY D. ROTHSTEIN (Bar No. CA 143157)
One Embarcadero Center, 30th Floor
San Francisco, CA 94111
Telephone: (415) 291-7400
Facsimile: (415) 291-7474

Attorneys for ~~Petitioner~~ Trustee,
BANK OF AMERICA, N.A.

FILED
San Francisco County Superior Court
MAY 16 2012
CLERK OF THE COURT
BY: [signature]
Deputy Clerk

SUPERIOR COURT OF THE STATE OF CALIFORNIA

FOR THE COUNTY OF SAN FRANCISCO

In the Matter of the Trust for Michael created under the Goodall Trust dated September 12, 1990.	Case No. PTR-99-273030 **~~[PROPOSED]~~ ORDER RESULTING FROM HEARING ON MAY 7, 2012:** **(1) DENYING THE AMENDED PETITION OF SAM SLOAN FOR FORENSIC DOCUMENT EXAMINATION OF DOCUMENTS PURPORTED TO BE TRUST DOCUMENTS OF THE GOODALL FAMILY TRUST; AND** **(2) GRANTING BANK OF AMERICA, N.A.'S PETITION FOR DETERMINATION OF THE BENEFICIARIES TO WHOM TRUST PROPERTY SHALL PASS UPON TERMINATION OF TRUST** Hearing Date: May 7, 2012 Time: 9:00 a.m. Dept.: Probate (Room 204)

The following matters came on for hearing on May 7, 2012, at 9:00 a.m. in the Probate Department (Room 204) of the above-entitled Court, the Honorable Peter J. Busch, presiding: (a) Bank of America, N.A.'s Petition for Determination of the Beneficiaries to Whom Trust Property Shall Pass Upon Termination of Trust (the "Petition for Determination of Beneficiaries"); (b) Samuel Sloan's Objection to Petition for Determination of Beneficiaries and Request for Continuance of Hearing; (c) the Further Probate Opposition/Objection to Petition for

Determination of the Beneficiaries to Whom Trust Property Shall Pass Upon Termination of Trust Filed by Objector Samuel H. Sloan; (d) Samuel Sloan's Supplemental Objections to Petition for Determination of Beneficiaries and Request for Continuance of Hearing; (e) Petitioner Bank of America, N.A.'s Reply in Support of Petition for Determination of the Beneficiaries to Whom Trust Property Shall Pass upon Termination of Trust; (f) Sam Sloan's Further Supplemental Objections to Petition for Determination of Beneficiaries; (g) Sam Sloan's Objections to Evidence; (h) Guide Dogs for the Blind, Inc.'s Opposition to Sam Sloan's Further Supplemental Objections to Petition for Determination of Beneficiaries; (i) Petitioner Bank of America, N.A.'s Further Reply in Support of Petition for Determination of the Beneficiaries to Whom Trust Property Shall Pass Upon Termination of Trust; (j) Amended Petition of Sam Sloan for Forensic Document Examination of Documents Purported to be Trust Documents of the Goodall Family Trust (the "Amended Petition for Forensic Document Examination"); (k) Guide Dogs for the Blind, Inc.'s Opposition to Sam Sloan's Further Supplemental Objections to Petition for Determination of Beneficiaries; and (l) Petitioner Bank of America, N.A.'s Additional Reply in Support of Petition for Determination of the Beneficiaries to Whom Trust Property Shall Pass Upon Termination of Trust. Sam Ware appeared on behalf of Samuel Sloan. Alicia A. Adornato appeared on behalf of Guide Dogs for the Blind, Inc. Gary D. Rothstein appeared on behalf of Trustee, Bank of America, N.A. Samuel Sloan was present in the courtroom.

The Court finds the following:

(i) Notice of hearing of the Petition for Determination of Beneficiaries and notice of hearing of the Amended Petition for Forensic Document Examination have been given for the period of time and in the manner required by law;

(ii) Objections of Samuel Sloan to the validity of the Amendment to Goodall Trust dated August 24, 1994 (the "1994 Amendment") are time-barred under the statute of limitations of California Probate Code §16061.8. Consequently, good cause exists to overrule Samuel Sloan's objections to the validity of the 1994 Amendment. The 1994 Amendment is a valid, effective testamentary instrument executed by Kenneth F. Goodall and Rachel A. Goodall.

(iii) The production of the original 1994 Amendment is not necessary to determine the intent of Kenneth F. Goodall and Rachel A. Goodall with respect to the beneficiaries under the 1994 Amendment to whom the remainder of the Trust for Michael established under the 1994 Amendment shall pass due to the death of Michael Goodall because:

(a) The Notification by Trustee required under California Probate Code §16061.7 was served to Michael Goodall on October 5, 1999, and such Notification included the required warning advising Michael Goodall of the 120-day time period in which to challenge the validity of the 1994 Amendment;

(b) The 120-day time period in which to challenge the validity of the 1994 Amendment as prescribed by California Probate Code §16061.8 expired prior to Samuel Sloan asserting objections to the validity of the 1994 Amendment;

(c) Michael Goodall effectively adopted the 1994 Amendment when, in 1999 and 2000, respectively, he filed in this proceeding his Petition Re Determination That Particular Action By Beneficiary Does Not Constitute A Contest and his Petition for Removal of Trustee; and

(d) The original 1994 Amendment cannot say anything more relevant about the intent of Kenneth F. Goodall and Rachel A. Goodall with respect to the beneficiaries of the Trust for Michael than can a copy of the 1994 Amendment.

(iv) The best interpretation of the provisions of the 1994 Amendment with respect to determining the beneficiaries to whom the remaining assets of the Trust for Michael established thereunder shall pass due to the death of Michael Goodall, and of the intent of Kenneth F. Goodall and Rachel A. Goodall with respect to whom such beneficiaries are, is set forth in the Petition for Determination of Beneficiaries, to wit: such beneficiaries are determined pursuant to Section 6.3(d) of the 1994 Amendment, as follows:

(a) Twenty thousand dollars ($20,000) to each of the then living brothers and sisters of the trustor, RACHEL A. GOODALL;

(b) The remaining assets of the Trust for Michael to Guide Dogs for the Blind of Marin, Inc. of San Rafael, California.

///

IT IS THEREFORE ORDERED, JUDGED AND DECREED THAT:

1. The Amended Petition for Forensic Document Examination is denied.

2. The Petition for Determination of Beneficiaries is granted.

3. The Trust for Michael shall be distributed pursuant to Section 6.3(d) of the 1994 Amendment, as follows:

(a) Twenty thousand dollars ($20,000) to each of the then living brothers and sisters of the trustor, RACHEL A. GOODALL;

(b) The remaining assets of the Trust for Michael to Guide Dogs for the Blind of Marin, Inc. of San Rafael, California.

APPROVED AS TO FORM AND SUBSTANCE:

Dated: May 11, 2012

Manatt, Phelps, & Phillips, LLP

By: [signature]
Gary D. Rothstein
Attorneys for Bank of America, N.A., Trustee

Dated: ____________________

____
Sam Ware
Attorney for Samuel Sloan

Dated: ____________________

Reed Smith LLP

By: ____________________
Alicia A. Adornato
Attorneys for Guide Dogs for the Blind, Inc.

Date: ____________________

____
Judge of the Superior Court

IT IS THEREFORE ORDERED, JUDGED AND DECREED THAT:

1. The Amended Petition for Forensic Document Examination is denied.

2. The Petition for Determination of Beneficiaries is granted.

3. The Trust for Michael shall be distributed pursuant to Section 6.3(d) of the 1994 Amendment, as follows:

(a) Twenty thousand dollars ($20,000) to each of the then living brothers and sisters of the trustor, RACHEL A. GOODALL;

(b) The remaining assets of the Trust for Michael to Guide Dogs for the Blind of Marin, Inc. of San Rafael, California.

APPROVED AS TO FORM ~~AND SUBSTANCE~~:

Dated: ______________________ Manatt, Phelps, & Phillips, LLP

By: ______________________
Gary D. Rothstein
Attorneys for Bank of America, N.A., Trustee

Dated: 5/ ______________________

____
Sam Ware
Attorney for Samuel Sloan

Dated: ______________________ Reed Smith LLP

By: ______________________
Alicia A. Adornato
Attorneys for Guide Dogs for the Blind, Inc.

Date: ______________________ ______________________

Judge of the Superior Court

IT IS THEREFORE ORDERED, JUDGED AND DECREED THAT:

1. The Amended Petition for Forensic Document Examination is denied.

2. The Petition for Determination of Beneficiaries is granted.

3. The Trust for Michael shall be distributed pursuant to Section 6.3(d) of the 1994 Amendment, as follows:

(a) Twenty thousand dollars ($20,000) to each of the then living brothers and sisters of the trustor, RACHEL A. GOODALL;

(b) The remaining assets of the Trust for Michael to Guide Dogs for the Blind of Marin, Inc. of San Rafael, California.

APPROVED AS TO FORM AND SUBSTANCE:

Dated: ______________________

Manatt, Phelps, & Phillips, LLP

By: ______________________
Gary D. Rothstein
Attorneys for Bank of America, N.A., Trustee

Dated: ______________________

____
Sam Ware
Attorney for Samuel Sloan

Dated: May 10, 2012

Reed Smith LLP

By: [signature]
Alicia A. Adornato
Attorneys for Guide Dogs for the Blind, Inc.

Date: 5/15/2012

[signature]
Judge of the Superior Court

MANATT, PHELPS & PHILLIPS, LLP
ATTORNEYS AT LAW
SAN FRANCISCO

Exhibit B

Order of San Francisco Superior Court dated September 27, 2012

MANATT, PHELPS & PHILLIPS, LLP
GARY D. ROTHSTEIN (Bar No. CA 143157)
One Embarcadero Center, 30th Floor
San Francisco, CA 94111
Telephone: (415) 291-7400
Facsimile: (415) 291-7474

Attorneys for Petitioner,
BANK OF AMERICA, N.A.

ENDORSED
FILED
San Francisco County Superior Court

SEP 27 2012

CLERK OF THE COURT
By: NOELIA RIVERA
Deputy Clerk

SUPERIOR COURT OF THE STATE OF CALIFORNIA

FOR THE COUNTY OF SAN FRANCISCO

In the Matter of the Trust for Michael created under the Goodall Trust dated September 12, 1990.	Case No. PTR-99-273030 **~~[PROPOSED~~] ORDER DENYING SAM SLOAN'S AMENDED NOTICE OF MOTION AND MOTION TO RECONSIDER [ERRONEOUSLY CAPTIONED EARLIER AS MOTION TO COMPEL PRODUCTION OF DOCUMENTS]** Hearing Date: July 19, 2012 Time: 2:00 p.m. Dept.: Probate (Room 204)

The following matters came on for hearing on July 19, 2012, at 2:00 p.m. in the Probate Department (Room 204) of the above-entitled Court, the Honorable Peter J. Busch, presiding: (a) Sam Sloan's Notice of Motion and Motion to Reconsider [Erroneously Captioned Earlier as Motion to Compel Production of Documents] and Declaration of Sloan in Support Thereof ("Sloan's Motion to Reconsider"); (b) Declaration of David S. Moore; (c) Bank of America, N.A.'s Opposition to Sam Sloan's Amended Notice of Motion and Motion to Reconsider [Erroneously Captioned Earlier as Motion to Compel Production of Documents]; (d) Declaration of Gary D. Rothstein in Support of Bank of America, N.A.'S Opposition to Sam Sloan's Amended Notice of Motion and Motion for Reconsideration; (e) Guide Dogs for the Blind, Inc.'s Joinder in Bank of America, N.A.'s Response to Sam Sloan's Motion to Reconsider;

and (f) Sam Sloan's Reply Memorandum Regarding Motion to Reconsider, and Declaration of Sam Ware in support thereof. Sam Ware appeared on behalf of Samuel Sloan. Alicia A. Adornato appeared on behalf of Guide Dogs for the Blind, Inc. Gary D. Rothstein appeared on behalf of Trustee, Bank of America, N.A. Samuel Sloan was present in the courtroom.

On July 18, 2012, the Court issued a Tentative Ruling with respect to the foregoing documents, which stated, in relevant part, as follows:

> "The Motion to Reconsider (mistitled as "Motion to Compel Production of Documents and Further Deposition") is denied. The moving party has not presented new facts or circumstances within the meaning of C.C.P. section 1008, and, in any event, to the extent any of moving party's submissions was properly considered new facts or circumstances, it would not lead the Court to change its ruling."

Having considered the foregoing documents, all papers submitted in support thereof, all papers submitted in opposition thereof, all other papers in the Court file in this matter, and the argument of counsel presented at the hearing, the Court makes the following findings:

(i) Notice of hearing of Sloan's Motion to Reconsider has been given for the period of time and in the manner required by law;

(ii) Good cause exists to adopt the Tentative Ruling as the Court's final order; and

(iii) Good cause does not exist for the Court to impose sanctions against Sam Sloan or Sam Ware at this time.

///

///

///

///

///

///

///

///

///

IT IS THEREFORE ORDERED, JUDGED AND DECREED THAT:

1. Sloan's Motion to Reconsider is denied; and

2. No sanctions are imposed at this time.

APPROVED AS TO FORM AND SUBSTANCE:

Dated: July 27, 2012 — Manatt, Phelps, & Phillips, LLP

By: Gary D. Rothstein
Gary D. Rothstein
Attorneys for Bank of America, N.A., Trustee

Dated: ____________________

____
Sam Ware
Attorney for Samuel Sloan

Dated: ____________________ — Reed Smith LLP

By: ____________________
Alicia A. Adornato
Attorneys for Guide Dogs for the Blind, Inc.

Date: ____________________

____
Judge of the Superior Court

IT IS THEREFORE ORDERED. JUDGED AND DECREED THAT:

1. Sloan's Motion to Reconsider is denied: and

2. No sanctions are imposed at this time.

APPROVED AS TO FORM AND SUBSTANCE:

Dated: ____________________ Manatt. Phelps, & Phillips. LLP

By: ____________________
Gary D. Rothstein
Attorneys for Bank of America, N.A., Trustee

Dated: 7/27/12 ____________________
Sam Ware
Attorney for Samuel Sloan

Dated: ____________________ Reed Smith LLP

By: ____________________
Alicia A. Adornato
Attorneys for Guide Dogs for the Blind, Inc.

Date: ____________________ ____________________
Judge of the Superior Court

IT IS THEREFORE ORDERED, JUDGED AND DECREED THAT:

1. Sloan's Motion to Reconsider is denied; and

2. No sanctions are imposed at this time.

APPROVED AS TO FORM AND SUBSTANCE:

Dated: ____________________ Manatt, Phelps, & Phillips, LLP

By: ____________________
Gary D. Rothstein
Attorneys for Bank of America, N.A., Trustee

Dated: ____________________ ____________________
Sam Ware
Attorney for Samuel Sloan

Dated: July 27, 2012 Reed Smith LLP

By: Alicia Adornato
Alicia A. Adornato
Attorneys for Guide Dogs for the Blind, Inc.

Date: 9/26/2012 PETER J. BUSCH
____
Judge of the Superior Court

Exhibit C

Order of San Francisco Superior Court dated November 15, 2012

MC-053

ATTORNEY OR PARTY WITHOUT ATTORNEY *(Name, state bar number, and address)*:	FOR COURT USE ONLY
Sam Ware 105005 700 Larkspur Landing Cir #199 Larkspur CA 94939 TELEPHONE NO.: 415 464 4872 FAX NO. *(Optional)*: E-MAIL ADDRESS *(Optional)*: ATTORNEY FOR *(Name)*: pro per	**FILED** Superior Court of California County of San Francisco NOV 15 2012 CLERK OF THE COURT BY: Rosie Nogura Deputy Clerk
SUPERIOR COURT OF CALIFORNIA, COUNTY OF San Francisco STREET ADDRESS: 400 McAllister St MAILING ADDRESS: CITY AND ZIP CODE: San Francisco CA BRANCH NAME:	
CASE NAME: In Re Goodall Trust	CASE NUMBER: PTR 99 273030
ORDER GRANTING ATTORNEY'S MOTION TO BE RELIEVED AS COUNSEL—CIVIL	HEARING DATE: October 29, 2012 DEPT.: 204 TIME: 10:30 am BEFORE HON.: Peter Busch DATE ACTION FILED: 12/21/99 TRIAL DATE: none

1. The motion of *(name of attorney)*: Sam Ware
   to be relieved as counsel of record for *(name of client)*: Samuel Sloan
   a party to this action or proceeding, came on regularly for hearing at the date, time, and place indicated above.

2. The following persons were present at the hearing:
   Sam Ware, Samuel Sloan, and Arden Van Upp

FINDINGS

3. Attorney has
   a. ☐ personally served the client with papers in support of this motion.
   b. ☑ served client by mail and submitted a declaration establishing that the service requirements of California Rules of Court, rule 3.1362, have been satisfied.

4. Attorney has shown sufficient reasons why the motion to be relieved as counsel should be granted and why the attorney has brought a motion under Code of Civil Procedure section 284(2) instead of filing a consent under section 284(1).

ORDER

5. Attorney is relieved as counsel of record for client
   a. ☐ effective upon the filing of the proof of service of this signed order upon the client.
   b. ☑ effective on *(specify date)*: 10/29/2012

6. The client's ☑ current ☐ last known address and telephone number:
   461 Peachstone Ter., San Rafael CA 94930 (415) 419-5980

If the client's current address is known, service on the client must hereafter be made at that address unless otherwise ordered in item 13. If the current address is not known, service must be made according to Code of Civil Procedure section 1011 (b) and rule 3.252 of the California Rules of Court.

7. a. The next scheduled hearing in this action or proceeding is set for *(date, time, and place)*:
   PJB November 15 2012 Dept 204 of the above Court
   b. The hearing will concern *(subject matter)*:
   Motion for Sanctions

NOTICE TO CLIENT
You or your new attorney, if any, must prepare for and attend this hearing.

CASE NAME: In Re Goodall Trust	CASE NUMBER: PTR 99 273030

8. The following additional hearings and other proceedings (including discovery matters) are set in this action *(describe the date, time, place, and subject matter of each):*
none

9. The trial in this action or proceeding:
a. ☑ is not yet set.
b. ☐ is set for *(specify date, time, and place):*

10. Client is hereby notified of the following effects this order may have upon parties.

NOTICE TO CLIENT

Your present attorney will no longer be representing you. You may not in most cases represent yourself if you are one of the parties on the following list:

- A guardian
- A conservator
- A trustee
- A personal representative
- A probate fiduciary
- A corporation
- A guardian ad litem
- An unincorporated association

If you are one of these parties, YOU SHOULD IMMEDIATELY SEEK LEGAL ADVICE REGARDING LEGAL REPRESENTATION. Failure to retain an attorney may lead to an order striking the pleadings or to the entry of a default judgment.

11. Client is notified that, if the client will be representing himself or herself, the client shall be solely responsible for the case.

NOTICE TO CLIENT WHO WILL BE UNREPRESENTED

You will not have an attorney representing you. You may wish to seek legal assistance. If you do not have a new attorney to represent you in this action or proceeding, and you are legally permitted to do so, you will be representing yourself. It will be your responsibility to comply with all court rules and applicable laws. If you fail to do so, or fail to appear at hearings, action may be taken against you. You may lose your case.

12. Client is notified that it is the client's duty to keep the court informed at all times of the client's current address.

NOTICE TO CLIENT WHO WILL BE UNREPRESENTED

The court needs to know how to contact you. If you do not keep the court and other parties informed of your current address and telephone number, they will not be able to send you notices of actions that may affect you, including actions that may adversely affect your interests or result in your losing the case.

13. The court further orders *(specify):*

Date: 11/15/2012

Peter J B
JUDGE OR JUDICIAL OFFICER
PETER J. BUSCH

Exhibit D

Order of San Francisco Superior Court dated November 26, 2012

SAM WARE (State Bar No. 105005)
700 Larkspur Landing Circle, #199
Larkspur, CA 94939

Telephone 415-464-4872

E-mail sam@samware.us

Sanctions Respondent, Pro per

FILED
San Francisco County Superior Court

NOV 26 2012

CLERK OF THE COURT
By: [signature: Maria Rivera]
Deputy Clerk

SUPERIOR COURT OF THE STATE OF CALIFORNIA

COUNTY OF SAN FRANCISCO

In the Matter of the Trust for Michael created under the Goodall Trust dated September 12, 1990	Case No. PTR-99-273030 Order Denying Motion for Sanctions Hrg Date: November 15, 2012 Time: 2:00 PM Department: 204

The court having considered Bank of America's motion for sanctions on November 15, 2012,

It is hereby ordered that the motion is denied.

Date: 11/21/2012

[signature]
Judge of the Superior Court

Approved as to Form:

[signature]
Attorneys for Bank of America

Exhibit E

Register of Actions in Marin County Probate Court in Estate of K. Michael Goodall, Case No. 1100596

MARIN SUPERIOR COURT OF CALIFORNIA, COUNTY OF MARIN		
K. MICHAEL GOODALL, ESTATE OF Decedent(s) VS. Trustee(s)	DATE FILED:	2/1/2011
	CASE TYPE:	Probate
	CASE SUBTYPE:	Decedent - Estate
	DATE OF LAST ACTIVITY:	9/24/2012
	DATE/TIME RUN:	1/28/2013 11:50am
REGISTER OF ACTIONS	CASE NUMBER:	PRO 1100596

INVOLVED PERSON/PARTY AND ATTORNEY SUMMARY:

GOODALL, K. MICHAEL is the Decedent and is represented by:

BANK OF AMERICA N.A. is the Trustee and is represented by: ROTHSTEIN, GARY D.

SLOAN, SAMUEL H. is the Personal Representative and is represented by: PRO PER

GUIDE DOGS FOR THE BLIND, INC. is the Other and is represented by: ADORNATO, ALICIA

REGISTER OF ACTIONS:

2/1/2011 CASE OPEN / ACTIVE STATUS Hon. Verna A. Adams

2/1/2011 FILING FEE PROCESSED: PREP, SAMUEL SLOAN - 395.00

2/1/2011 COMPLAINT/FIRST PAPER PETITION FOR PROBATE OF WILL AND FOR LETTERS TESTAMENTARY. $395.00 PAID.

2/2/2011 HEARING CONFIRMED FOR: 03/07/2011 AT: 08:30 AM FOR APPEARANCE TYPE: PROB IN DEPARTMENT: D01

2/2/2011 HEARING CONFIRMED FOR: 02/01/2013 AT: 09:00 AM FOR APPEARANCE TYPE: CSCM IN DEPARTMENT: Z7

2/25/2011 PROOF OF PUBLICATION FILED MARINSCOPE; FEB.9, 16, AND 23, 2011

3/3/2011 DUTIES AND LIABILITIES OF PERSONAL REPRESENTATIVE FILED, BY SAMUEL H. SLOAN

3/7/2011 MINUTE ORDER POSTED - Appearance: 3/7/2011 at 08:30 AM for PETITION FOR PROBATE

JUDGE/PROTEM/REFEREE VERNA A. ADAMS , REPORTER NOT REPORTED , DEP CLK VITA JOHANSON

PLAINTIFF/PETITIONER SAMUEL SLOAN IS PRESENT IN PRO PER

TENTATIVE RULING CONTINUED.

CONTINUED TO MARCH 21, 2011 FOR NOTICE TO ALTERNATIVE EXECUTOR.

HEARING CONTINUED TO: 03/21/2011 AT: 08:30 AM FOR APPEARANCE TYPE: PROB IN DEPARTMENT: D01 FROM DATE: 03/07/2011 FROM TIME: 08:30 AM FROM APPEARANCE TYPE: PROB FROM DEPARTMENT: D01

ENTERED BY: VJ

3/15/2011 CREDITOR'S CLAIM BANK OF AMERICA: $14,451.19

3/15/2011 CREDITOR'S CLAIM BANK OF AMERICA: $11,109.61

3/21/2011 MINUTE ORDER POSTED - Appearance: 3/21/2011 at 08:30 AM for PETITION FOR PROBATE

JUDGE/PROTEM/REFEREE VERNA A. ADAMS , REPORTER CATHY HEEFNER , DEP CLK JULIE WITHEY

ATTORNEY SAMUEL H. SLOAN APPEARED FOR HIMSELF AS PERSONAL REPRESENTATIVE

APPEARANCE BY ROY HOPPE EXECUTOR

TENTATIVE RULING : APPEARANCE IS REQUIRED. IF THERE IS NO APPEARANCE THEN THE MATTER IS OFF CALENDAR

THE COURT NOTES THE PROOF OF SERVICE TO BANK OF AMERICA HAS BEEN FILED.

IT IS ORDERED: THE COURT ACCEPTS THE RESIGNATION OF MR. HOPPE AS EXECUTOR AND APPOINTS SAMUEL H. SLOAN.

THE TENTATIVE RULING IS AFFIRMED AND MADE FINAL.

ORDER SIGNED IN OPEN COURT

ENTERED BY: JW

3/21/2011 ORDER FOR PROBATE APPOINTING SAMUEL H. SLOAN ADMINISTRATOR WITH WILL ANNEXED WITH FULL AUTHORITY. SIGNED BY JUDGE VERNA A. ADAMS

3/21/2011 WILL DATED: 1/15/04 FILED

3/21/2011 LETTERS OF ADMINISTRATION WITH WILL ANNEXED WITH FULL AUTHORITY: SAMUEL H. SLOAN APPOINTED

3/29/2011 CREDITOR'S CLAIM $974.27 PACIFIC GAS AND ELECTRIC COMPANY

4/12/2011 HEARING CONFIRMED FOR: 08/24/2011 AT: 09:00 AM FOR APPEARANCE TYPE: PROB IN DEPARTMENT: Z8

4/12/2011 HEARING CONFIRMED FOR: 04/25/2012 AT: 09:00 AM FOR APPEARANCE TYPE: PROB IN DEPARTMENT: Z8

5/20/2011 HEARING CONFIRMED FOR: 05/20/2011 AT: 09:00 AM FOR APPEARANCE TYPE: PROB IN DEPARTMENT: D07

5/20/2011 MINUTE ORDER POSTED

EX PARTE MINUTE ORDER

JUDGE/PROTEM/REFEREE HARVEY E. GOLDFINE , REPORTER ELAINE NINKOVICH , DEP CLK CHRIS HAHN

APPEARANCE BY SAMUEL SLOAN, ADMINISTRATOR WITH WILL ANNEXED, PETITIONER.

APPEARANCE BY GARY ROTHSTEIN, TRUSTEE, BANK OF AMERICA, APPEARING BY COURT CALL.

APPEARANCE BY MATTHEW URBACH, TRUSTEE, BANK OF AMERICA. APPEARING BY COURT CALL.

NOTICE GIVEN AS REQUIRED BY LAW

MR. ROTHSTEIN REPORTS HE HAS RECEIVED A COPY OF THE PETITION AND TEMPORARY RESTRAINING ORDER WITH REGARD TO THE TRUST CREATED BY DECEDANT'S PARENTS FOR THE DECEDANT.

MR. ROTHSTEIN FURTHER REPORTS HE HAS BEEN INFORMED THAT THE PROPERTY WAS VACATED AND ITS CONTENTS, SOME OF WHICH ARE PART OF THE TRUST, WERE REMOVED AND PUT IN STORAGE AT AN AUCTION HOUSE.

MR. ROTHSTEIN STATES HIS BELIEF THAT THE HOME IS AN ASSET OF THE TRUST. THIS MATTER IS GOING TO BE HEARD IN THE SAN FRANCISCO COUNTY SUPERIOR COURT ON MAY 25, 2011.

MR. ROTHSTEIN HAS NO OBJECTION TO ORDER SHORTENING TIME.

MR. SLOAN REPORTS THAT PROPERTY BELONGING TO ROY HOPPE, AN ALLEGED BENEFICIARY OF THE WILL, WAS REMOVED AND THAT MR. HOPPE IS NOW HOMELESS.

MR. SLOAN STATES HE RECEIVED NO NOTICE OF INTENT TO REMOVE PROPERTY FROM THE HOME AND, IN HIS OPINION, ANY LEGAL ACTION MUST BE TAKEN IN THE COUNTY WHERE THE PROPERTY IS LOCATED.

THE COURT MAKES THE FOLLOWING FINDINGS AND ORDERS:

COURT GRANTS ORDER SHORTENING TIME.

COURT INFORMS MR. SLOAN THAT IT IS HIS RESPONSIBILITY TO SUBMIT ORDER SHORTENING TIME AND CITATION TO THE AUCTION HOUSE.

THIS MATTER IS CONTINUED TO JUNE 13, 2011 AT 8:30 AM IN DEPARTMENT "H" BEFORE JUDGE ADAMS FOR CONSIDERATION OF RESTRAINING ORDER AND FURTHER PROCEEDINGS.

HEARING CONTINUED TO: 06/13/2011 AT: 08:30 AM FOR APPEARANCE TYPE: PROB IN DEPARTMENT: D01 FROM DATE: 05/20/2011 FROM TIME: 09:00 AM FROM APPEARANCE TYPE: PROB FROM DEPARTMENT: D07

	MR. ROTHSTEIN ACCEPTS SERVICE OF NOTICE AS TO NEXT HEARING ON BEHALF OF BANK OF AMERICA. ENTERED BY: CHRIS HAHN
5/25/2011	IT IS ORDERED: ORDER SHORTENING TIME ON PREP'S MTN. TO RECOVER ESTATE PROPERTY TO BE HEARD ON 6/13/11 AT 8:30AM IN DEPT. H. SIGNED BY COMM. HARVEY E. GOLDFINE
6/13/2011	MINUTE ORDER POSTED - Appearance: 6/13/2011 at 08:30 AM for OTHER JUDGE/PROTEM/REFEREE VERNA A. ADAMS , REPORTER NOT REPORTED , DEP CLK J. CHARIFA APPEARANCE BY PERSONAL REPRESENTATIVE, SAM SLOAN. APPEARANCE BY ROY HOPPE, BENEFECIARY OF THE ESTATE. COUNSEL INDICATES THAT PROPERTY HAS BEEN RETURNED. IT IS ORDERED: OFF CALENDAR. MATTER HAS BEEN RESOLVED. ISSUES RAISED BY MR. SLOAN REGARDING RACHEL GOODALL AND THE DIFFICULTY OF RETAINING INFORMATION FROM BANK OF AMERICA ON THE STATUS OF THE MONEY, ARE NOT BEFORE THE COURTAT THIS TIME. MR. SLOAN IS DIRECTED TO FILE AN APPROPRIATE PETITION WITH THE COURT IF HE WISHES TO PURSUE THESE ISSUES. ENTERED BY: JC
6/30/2011	HEARING CONFIRMED FOR: 09/26/2011 AT: 08:30 AM FOR APPEARANCE TYPE: PROB IN DEPARTMENT: D01
8/2/2011	HEARING CONFIRMED FOR: 08/22/2011 AT: 08:30 AM FOR APPEARANCE TYPE: PROB IN DEPARTMENT: D01
8/22/2011	MINUTE ORDER POSTED - Appearance: 8/22/2011 at 08:30 AM for PETITION JUDGE/PROTEM/REFEREE VERNA A. ADAMS , REPORTER NOT REPORTED , DEP CLK VITA JOHANSON NO APPEARANCE BY OR FOR THE PARTIES THE MATTER IS NOT HEARD OR REPORTED. THE TENTATIVE RULING IS FINAL. RULING- IF NO OBJECTIONS ARE RAISED THEN THE MATTER IS PRE-GRANTED AND NO APPEARANCE IS NECESSARY. PETITION GRANTED. ENTERED BY: VJ
8/22/2011	IT IS ORDERED: ORDER ON PETITION FOR AUTHORITY TO ENTER INTO CONTINGENCY FEE AGREEMENT GRANTED. SIGNED BY JUDGE VERNA A. ADAMS
9/6/2011	APPEARANCE MOVED TO: 10/26/2011 AT: 09:00 AM FOR APPEARANCE TYPE: PROB IN DEPARTMENT: Z8 MOVE REASON: * FROM DATE: 08/24/2011 FROM TIME: 09:00 AM FROM APPEARANCE TYPE: PROB FROM DEPARTMENT: Z8
9/22/2011	HEARING CONFIRMED FOR: 12/27/2011 AT: 08:30 AM FOR APPEARANCE TYPE: PROB IN DEPARTMENT: D01
9/22/2011	FILING FEE PROCESSED: TRUS, BANK OF AMERICA N.A. - 395.00
9/22/2011	DEMURRER TO SAMUEL H. SLOAN'S PETITION UNDER CA. PROB. CODE SEC. 850 TO RECOVER ESTATE PROPERTY FILED BY BANK OF AMERICA, N.A.. $395.00 PAID.
9/26/2011	MINUTE ORDER POSTED - Appearance: 9/26/2011 at 08:30 AM for PETITION JUDGE/PROTEM/REFEREE COMM. RANDOLPH E. HEUBACH , REPORTER NOT REPORTED , DEP CLK G. COMPTON

APPEARANCE BY SAMUEL SLOAN

APPEARANCE BY BENEFICIARIES OF THE ESTATE, FRANK THORNALLY AND ROY HOPPE

SAMUEL SLOAN CALLED OBJECTS TO THE COURT'S TENTATIVE RULING.

MR. SLOAN REQUESTS FOR AN ACCOUNTING OF THE FUNDS.

THE COURT NOTES THAT THERE'S A PENDING TRUST ACTION IN SAN FRANCISCO AND THE DEMURRER NEEDS TO BE RESOLVED BEFORE THIS PETITIONER IS HEARD.

IT IS ORDERED: MATTER CONTINUED TO 12/27/11 @ 8:30 A.M. TO POTENTIALLY BE SET FOLLOWING RULING ON DERMURRER.

THE TENTATIVE RULING IS AFFIRMED AND MADE FINAL.

TENTATIVE RULING CONTINUED.

ENTERED BY: G. COMPTON

11/10/2011 APPEARANCE MOVED TO: 05/09/2012 AT: 09:00 AM FOR APPEARANCE TYPE: PROB IN DEPARTMENT: Z8 MOVE REASON: * FROM DATE: 10/26/2011 FROM TIME: 09:00 AM FROM APPEARANCE TYPE: PROB FROM DEPARTMENT: Z8

11/10/2011 APPEARANCE MOVED TO: 07/11/2012 AT: 09:00 AM FOR APPEARANCE TYPE: PROB IN DEPARTMENT: Z8 MOVE REASON: * FROM DATE: 04/25/2012 FROM TIME: 09:00 AM FROM APPEARANCE TYPE: PROB FROM DEPARTMENT: Z8

12/27/2011 MINUTE ORDER POSTED - Appearance: 12/27/2011 at 08:30 AM for MOTION

JUDGE/PROTEM/REFEREE COMM. RANDOLPH E. HEUBACH , REPORTER MAUREEN STEGER , DEP CLK G. COMPTON

APPEARANCE BY ADMINISTRATOR, SAMUEL SLOAN

NO APPEARANCE BY OR FOR THE TRUSTEE, BANK OF AMERICA

MR. SLOAN OBJECTS TO THE CONTINUANCE OF HIS MOTION FOR TO RECOVER ESTATE PROPERTY AND REQUESTS FOR HIS PETITION TO BE GRANTED. STATES THAT HE ONLY AGREED TO THE CONTINUANCE FOR THE DEMURRER.

TENTATIVE RULING CONTINUED.

IT IS ORDERED: CASE IS CONTINUED TO 02/21/12 @ 8:30 A.M. BY STIPULATION.

HEARING CONTINUED TO: 02/21/2012 AT: 08:30 AM FOR APPEARANCE TYPE: PROB IN DEPARTMENT: D01 FROM DATE: 12/27/2011 FROM TIME: 08:30 AM FROM APPEARANCE TYPE: PROB FROM DEPARTMENT: D01

ENTERED BY: G. COMPTON

2/21/2012 MINUTE ORDER POSTED - Appearance: 2/21/2012 at 08:30 AM for MOTION

DEPARTMENT H MATTER CALENDARED IN DEPARTMENT A.

JUDGE/PROTEM/REFEREE HARVEY E. GOLDFINE , REPORTER NOT REPORTED , DEP CLK CHRIS HAHN

NO APPEARANCE BY OR FOR THE PARTIES

TENTATIVE RULING: CONTINUED TO 3-19-2012 AT 8:30 AM BY STIPULATION.

HEARING CONTINUED TO: 03/19/2012 AT: 08:30 AM FOR APPEARANCE TYPE: PROB IN DEPARTMENT: D01 FROM DATE: 02/21/2012 FROM TIME: 08:30 AM FROM APPEARANCE TYPE: PROB FROM DEPARTMENT: D01

ENTERED BY: CHRIS HAHN

3/6/2012 FILING FEE PROCESSED: OTHR, GUIDE DOGS FOR THE BLIND, INC. - 395.00

3/6/2012 OPPOSITION TO MOTION FOR ORDER TO RELEASE LODGED DOCUMENTS PURPORTED TO BE THE ORIGINAL WILLS DECEDENTS KENNETH F. GOODALL AND RACHEL A. GOODALL FOR FORENSIC DOCUMENT EXAMINATION FILED BY GUIDE DOGS FOR THE BLIND, INC. $395.00 PAID.

3/15/2012 REPLY TO BANK OF AMERICA'S ATTEMPT AT DEMURRER FILED BY SAMUEL H. SLOAN.

3/19/2012 MINUTE ORDER POSTED - Appearance: 3/19/2012 at 08:30 AM for MOTION

JUDGE/PROTEM/REFEREE VERNA A. ADAMS , REPORTER NOT REPORTED , DEP CLK VITA JOHANSON

NO APPEARANCE BY OR FOR THE PARTIES

TENTATIVE RULING CONTINUED.

IT IS ORDERED: CONTINUED TO APRIL 2, 2012 FOR FURTHER REVIEW

HEARING CONTINUED TO: 04/02/2012 AT: 08:30 AM FOR APPEARANCE TYPE: PROB IN DEPARTMENT: D01 FROM DATE: 03/19/2012 FROM TIME: 08:30 AM FROM APPEARANCE TYPE: PROB FROM DEPARTMENT: D01

ENTERED BY: VJ

3/22/2012 IT IS ORDERED: ORDER TO CONTINUE HEARING FROM 4/2/12 TO 4/16/12 GRANTED. SIGNED BY JUDGE VERNA A. ADAMS

4/2/2012 MINUTE ORDER POSTED - Appearance: 4/2/2012 at 08:30 AM for MOTION

JUDGE/PROTEM/REFEREE VERNA A. ADAMS , REPORTER NOT REPORTED , DEP CLK VITA JOHANSON

NO APPEARANCE BY OR FOR THE PARTIES

TENTATIVE RULING CONTINUED.

IT IS ORDERED: CONTINUED TO APRIL 16, 2012 BY STIPULATION

HEARING CONTINUED TO: 04/16/2012 AT: 08:30 AM FOR APPEARANCE TYPE: PROB IN DEPARTMENT: D01 FROM DATE: 04/02/2012 FROM TIME: 08:30 AM FROM APPEARANCE TYPE: PROB FROM DEPARTMENT: D01

ENTERED BY: VJ

4/16/2012 MINUTE ORDER POSTED - Appearance: 4/16/2012 at 08:30 AM for MOTION

JUDGE/PROTEM/REFEREE VERNA A. ADAMS , REPORTER NOT REPORTED , DEP CLK VITA JOHANSON

ATTORNEY ALICIA ADORNATO APPEARED FOR GUIDE DOGS FOR THE BLIND

ATTORNEY GARY ROTHSTEIN APPEARED FOR TRUSTEE BANK OF AMERICA

APPEARANCE BY ADMINISTRATOR SAMUEL SLOAN, SELF REPRESENTED LITIGANT

MATTER COMES BEFORE THE COURT ON AN APPEARANCE IS REQUIRED TENTATIVE RULING

THE MATTER IS HEARD AND ARGUED

MATTER IS SUBMITTED

BANK OF AMERICA'S REQUEST FOR JUDICIAL NOTICE FILED 09-22-2011 IS GRANTED, PER EVIDENCE CODE SECTIONS 452 AND 453.

IT IS ORDERED: THE DEMURRER IS SUSTANED WITHOUT LEAVE TO AMEND AND THE SECTION 850 PETITION IS DENIED WITHOUT PREJUDICE.

	THE MOTION FOR AN ORDER TO RELEASE DOCUMENTS TO A FORENSIC DOCUMENT EXAMINER: THAT MOTION IS DENIED. PETITION DENIED. CASE DISPOSED IN ENTIRETY CASE RE-OPENED / ACTIVE (CASE DISPOSED ENTRY IS CLERICAL ERROR) ENTERED BY: VJ
4/26/2012	IT IS ORDERED: ORDER RESULTING FROM HEARING ON APRIL 16, 2012 GRANTED. SIGNED BY JUDGE VERNA A. ADAMS (SEE FILE FOR FULL DETAILS OF ORDER)
5/15/2012	APPEARANCE MOVED TO: 09/19/2012 AT: 09:00 AM FOR APPEARANCE TYPE: PROB IN DEPARTMENT: Z8 MOVE REASON: * FROM DATE: 05/09/2012 FROM TIME: 09:00 AM FROM APPEARANCE TYPE: PROB FROM DEPARTMENT: Z8
9/24/2012	APPEARANCE MOVED TO: 11/14/2012 AT: 09:00 AM FOR APPEARANCE TYPE: PROB IN DEPARTMENT: Z8 MOVE REASON: * FROM DATE: 09/19/2012 FROM TIME: 09:00 AM FROM APPEARANCE TYPE: PROB FROM DEPARTMENT: Z8

Exhibit F

Register of Actions in Marin County Superior Court Unlawful Detainer Proceedings Case Numbers Civ 1203665 and Civ 1204541 and Order of Dismissal

MARIN SUPERIOR COURT OF CALIFORNIA, COUNTY OF MARIN		
BANK OF AMERICA, N.A. Plaintiff(s) VS. SAMUEL H. SLOAN, ET. AL. Defendant(s)	DATE FILED:	8/8/2012
	CASE TYPE:	Civil Complaint
	CASE SUBTYPE:	Unlawful Detainer
	DATE OF LAST ACTIVITY:	12/31/2012
	DATE/TIME RUN:	1/28/2013 12:02pm
REGISTER OF ACTIONS	CASE NUMBER:	CIV 1203665

INVOLVED PERSON/PARTY AND ATTORNEY SUMMARY:

BANK OF AMERICA, N.A. is the Plaintiff and is represented by: LOPEZ, ZAHER ; ROTHSTEIN, GARY D.

SLOAN, SAMUEL H. is the Defendant and is represented by: PRO PER

HOPPE, ROY is the Defendant and is represented by: PRO PER

THORNALLY, FRANK is the Defendant and is represented by: PRO PER

KIMURA, KAYO is the Defendant and is represented by: PRO PER

REGISTER OF ACTIONS:

8/8/2012	CASE OPEN / ACTIVE STATUS Hon. Roy O. Chernus
8/8/2012	CASE MARKED AS CONFIDENTIAL
8/8/2012	FULL NAME OF PLAINTIFF: BANK OF AMERICA, N.A., TRUSTEE OF THE TRUST FOR MICHAEL CREATED UNDER THE GOODALL TRUST DATED SEPTEMBER 12, 1990
8/8/2012	FILING FEE PROCESSED: PLTF, BANK OF AMERICA, N.A. - 240.00
8/8/2012	COMPLAINT/FIRST PAPER AMOUNT DOES NOT EXCEED $10,000
8/8/2012	SUMMONS ISSUED AND FILED
8/9/2012	AMENDED COMPLAINT FILED (1ST) BY ATTY GARY ROTHSTEIN; ZAHER LOPEZ OBO PLTF. (NO ADDL PARTIES)
8/9/2012	SUMMONS ISSUED (1ST AMENDED) AND FILED
8/9/2012	HEARING CONFIRMED FOR: 12/31/2012 AT: 08:30 AM FOR APPEARANCE TYPE: OSCH IN DEPARTMENT: D06
8/9/2012	HEARING CONFIRMED FOR: 12/31/2013 AT: 09:00 AM FOR APPEARANCE TYPE: CSCM IN DEPARTMENT: Z7
8/17/2012	ANSWER DEFT, SAMUEL SLOAN
8/17/2012	FILING FEE PROCESSED: DEFT, SAMUEL SLOAN - 225.00
8/20/2012	UD PROPERTY LOCATION: 461 PEACHSTONE TERRACE SAN RAFAEL CA 94903
8/20/2012	ANSWER DEFT, KAYO KIMURA
8/20/2012	PAUPERIS FILING GRANTED DEFT, KAYO KIMURA
8/20/2012	ANSWER DEFT, FRANK THORNALLY
8/20/2012	PAUPERIS FILING GRANTED DEFT, FRANK THORNALLY
8/20/2012	ANSWER DEFT, ROY HOPPE
8/20/2012	PAUPERIS FILING GRANTED DEFT, ROY HOPPE
10/9/2012	CASE REMOVED AS CONFIDENTIAL
10/9/2012	PAST 60 DAY LIMIT
12/31/2012	MINUTE ORDER POSTED - Appearance: 12/31/2012 at 08:30 AM for OSC RE: DISMISSAL JUDGE/PROTEM/REFEREE ROY O. CHERNUS , REPORTER NOT REPORTED , DEP CLK D.THAI NO APPEARANCE BY OR FOR THE PARTIES

MARIN SUPERIOR COURT OF CALIFORNIA, COUNTY OF MARIN		
BANK OF AMERICA, N.A. Plaintiff(s) VS. SAMUEL H. SLOAN, ET. AL. Defendant(s)	DATE FILED:	8/8/2012
	CASE TYPE:	Civil Complaint
	CASE SUBTYPE:	Unlawful Detainer
	DATE OF LAST ACTIVITY:	12/31/2012
	DATE/TIME RUN:	1/28/2013 12:02pm
REGISTER OF ACTIONS	CASE NUMBER:	CIV 1203665

IT IS ORDERED:

CASE DISPOSED BEFORE TRIAL; DISMISSED - OTHER REASONS WITHOUT PREJUDICE

CASE DISPOSED IN ENTIRETY

ENTERED BY: D.THAI

MARIN SUPERIOR COURT OF CALIFORNIA, COUNTY OF MARIN		
BANK OF AMERICA, N.A. Plaintiff(s) VS. SAMUEL H. SLOAN, ET AL Defendant(s)	DATE FILED:	10/9/2012
	CASE TYPE:	Civil Complaint
	CASE SUBTYPE:	Unlawful Detainer
	DATE OF LAST ACTIVITY:	12/10/2012
	DATE/TIME RUN:	1/28/2013 12:02pm
REGISTER OF ACTIONS	CASE NUMBER:	CIV 1204541

INVOLVED PERSON/PARTY AND ATTORNEY SUMMARY:

BANK OF AMERICA, N.A. is the Plaintiff and is represented by: ROTHSTEIN, GARY D.; URBACH, MATTHEW S.

SLOAN, SAMUEL H. is the Defendant and is represented by: PRO PER

HOPPE, ROY is the Defendant and is represented by: PRO PER

THORNALLY, FRANK is the Defendant and is represented by: PRO PER

KIMURA, KAYO is the Defendant and is represented by:

REGISTER OF ACTIONS:

10/9/2012	CASE OPEN / ACTIVE STATUS Hon. Roy O. Chernus
10/9/2012	NOTICE OF RERLATED CASE: CIV 1203665 BANK OF AMERICA, N.A., AS TRUSTEE VS SLOAN; HOPPE; THORNALLY; KIMURA; AND DOES 1 - 10
10/9/2012	CASE MARKED AS CONFIDENTIAL
10/9/2012	FILING FEE PROCESSED: PLTF, BANK OF AMERICA, N.A. - 240.00
10/9/2012	COMPLAINT/FIRST PAPER DOES NOT EXCEED $10,000
10/9/2012	SUMMONS ISSUED AND FILED
10/9/2012	FULL NAME PLTF: BANK OF AMERICA, N.A., TRUSTEE OF THE TRUST FOR MICHAEL CREATED UNDER THE GOODALL TRUST DATED 9/12/1990
10/9/2012	HEARING CONFIRMED FOR: 03/05/2013 AT: 08:30 AM FOR APPEARANCE TYPE: OSCH IN DEPARTMENT: D06
10/9/2012	HEARING CONFIRMED FOR: 04/09/2013 AT: 09:00 AM FOR APPEARANCE TYPE: CSCM IN DEPARTMENT: Z7
10/19/2012	UD PROPERTY LOCATION: 461 PEACHSTONE TERR SAN RAFAEL CA 94903
10/19/2012	ANSWER DEFT, SAMUEL SLOAN
10/19/2012	FILING FEE PROCESSED: DEFT, SAMUEL SLOAN - 225.00
10/19/2012	ANSWER DEFT, FRANK THORNALLY
10/19/2012	PAUPERIS FILING GRANTED DEFT, FRANK THORNALLY
10/22/2012	ANSWER DEFT, ROY HOPPE
10/22/2012	PAUPERIS FILING GRANTED DEFT, ROY HOPPE
10/22/2012	ANSWER DEFT, KAYO KIMURA
10/22/2012	PAUPERIS FILING GRANTED DEFT, KAYO KIMURA
10/23/2012	PROOF OF SERVICE FILED, AS TO: DEFT, KAYO KIMURA; BY PERSONAL SERVICE ON 10/10/12
10/23/2012	PROOF OF SERVICE FILED, AS TO: DEFT, SAMUEL H. SLOAN; BY PERSONAL SERVICE ON 10/10/12
10/23/2012	PROOF OF SERVICE TO ALL UNNAMED OCCPANTS; BY SERVING SAMUEL H. SLOAN AND POSTING ON 10/11/12
10/24/2012	PROOF OF SERVICE FILED, AS TO: DEFT, ROY HOPPE; BY SUBSTITUTED SERVICE ON KAYO KIMURA, CO-OCCUPANT ON 10-11-12 AND BY MAIL ON 10-12-12.

MARIN SUPERIOR COURT OF CALIFORNIA, COUNTY OF MARIN		
BANK OF AMERICA, N.A. Plaintiff(s) VS. SAMUEL H. SLOAN, ET AL Defendant(s)	DATE FILED:	10/9/2012
	CASE TYPE:	Civil Complaint
	CASE SUBTYPE:	Unlawful Detainer
	DATE OF LAST ACTIVITY:	12/10/2012
	DATE/TIME RUN:	1/28/2013 12:02pm
REGISTER OF ACTIONS	CASE NUMBER:	CIV 1204541

10/24/2012 PROOF OF SERVICE FILED, AS TO: DEFT, FRANK THORNALLY; BY SUBSTITUTED SERVICE ON 10-11-12 ON KAYO KIMURA, CO-OCCUPANT AND BY MAIL ON 10-12-12.

11/21/2012 APPEARANCE ADDED ON FOR: 11/28/2012 AT: 08:30 AM FOR APPEARANCE TYPE: LMCV IN DEPARTMENT: D06

11/28/2012 MINUTE ORDER POSTED - Appearance: 11/28/2012 at 08:30 AM for MOTION FOR SUMMARY JUDGMENT

JUDGE/PROTEM/REFEREE ROY O. CHERNUS , REPORTER PRIVATE CONTRACT REPORTEER, JO DILLINGHAM BREWER, CSR 9707 , DEP CLK S. DIENER

ATTORNEY EUGENE L. HAHN APPEARED FOR PLAINTIFF

DEFENDANT/RESPONDENT ROY HOPPE IS PRESENT IN PRO PER

DEFENDANT/RESPONDENT KAY KIMURA IS PRESENT IN PRO PER

DEFENDANT/RESPONDENT FRANK THORNALLY IS PRESENT IN PRO PER

DEFENDANT/RESPONDENT SAMUEL SLOAN AS ADMINISTRATOR OF THE GOODALL TRUST AND IS PRESENT IN PRO PER

MOTION(S) HEARD AND ARGUED

THE TENTATIVE RULING IS AFFIRMED AND MADE FINAL.

********* EXCEPT OF RULING, SEE COURT'S FILE FOR COMPLETE RULING ***********

MOTIONS FOR SUMMARY JUDGMENT BY PLAINTIFF BANK OF AMERICA, N.A., TRUSTEE OF THE TRUST FOR MICHAEL CREATED UNDER THE GOODALL TRUST DATED SEPTEMBER 21, 1990, AGAINST DEFENDANTS SAMUEL SLOAN, ROY HOPPE, FRANK THORNALLY, AND KAY KIMURA ARE DENIED.

HEARING BEFORE TRIAL

ENTERED BY: P. OKUBO

12/10/2012 CASE REMOVED AS CONFIDENTIAL

MARIN COUNTY SUPERIOR COURT
3501 Civic Center Drive, Room 113
P.O. Box 4988
San Rafael, CA 94913-4988

PLAINTIFF:
Bank of America N.A.

vs.

DEFENDANT:
Samuel H. Sloan Et Al

CASE NO. CIV 1203665

CIVIL MINUTES
ORDER TO SHOW CAUSE
Dismissal

CSCRT **JUDGE** Roy D. Chernus **DATE/TIME** 12-31-12 / 830 **CLERK** DT
APATT **ATTORNEY** ______ appeared for ______
APPPP **Plaintiff/Petitioner** ______ **is present in pro per.**
(APNAP) **No appearance by or for the parties.**
APNAB **No appearance by or for the** ______
CSMDT **THE COURT MODIFIES MANDATORY APPEARANCE DATES ON CASE MANAGEMENT SCHEDULE AS FOLLOWS: PREVIOUS DATES VACATED.**

Filing of Proof of Service ___/___/___ 8:30 / 9:00 a.m.
Filing of Answer or Default ___/___/___ 8:30 / 9:00 a.m.
Case Management Conference ___/___/___ 8:30 / 9:00 a.m.

FILED
DEC 31 2012
KIM TURNER
MARIN COUNTY SUPERIOR COURT

APOSC **ORDER TO SHOW CAUSE ISSUED FOR:**
(Name): ______
For Failing to Appear on ___/___/___ or file ☐ Proof of Service ☐ Request to Enter Default
As to ______

YOU ARE HEREBY ORDERED TO APPEAR IN COURT AS SET FORTH BELOW TO SHOW CAUSE WHY YOU FAILED TO COMPLY WITH THE STANDARD FILING REQUIREMENTS OF THE CASE MANAGEMENT SCHEDULE IN THE ABOVE REFERENCED CASE:
Date: ___/___/___ 8:30 / 9:00 a.m. Courtroom: ______ before Judge: ______

☐ FNSMS ☐ **SANCTIONS ARE TO BE PAID BY** ______ **TO THE MARIN COUNTY SUPERIOR COURT IN THE SUM OF $** ______ **BY** ___/___/___ **FOR:** ______

☐ CSTXT ______

☐ CSDLP **Case dismissed, lack of prosecution**
☒ CSDOT **Case disposed before trial; Dismissed, other reasons** Without prejudice
☒ CSDSP **Case disposed in its entirety**

Pltf to serve minute order

Roy O. Chernus
JUDGE OF THE SUPERIOR COURT

DECLARATION OF PERSONAL SERVICE/SERVICE BY MAIL
(Code of Civil Procedure Sections 1013a and 2015.5)

I, the undersigned, under penalty of perjury, declare that I am over 18 years of age, a citizen of the United States, an employee of the County of Marin and not a party to the action. I served this *Civil Minutes Order* by ☐ Personal Service, or ☒ Service by Mail (by placing true copies thereof, enclosed in a separate envelope, with postage fully prepaid by the filing party, in the United States Post Office mail box, at San Rafael, Marin County, California) on the date written herein, addressed to the parties/counsel as indicated on the complaint.

Zaler Lopez
11355 West Olympic Blvd
Los Angeles, CA 90064

Gary Rothstein
One Embarcadero Center 30th FL
San Francisco, CA 94111

Executed at San Rafael, California
1 / 2 / 13

KIM TURNER
Court Executive Officer
By: DTC

Exhibit G

Marin County Superior Court Unlawful Detainer Proceedings Case Numbers Civ 1204541 tentative ruling adopted as final ruling denying motion for summary judgment

SUPERIOR COURT OF CALIFORNIA
COUNTY OF MARIN

DATE: 11/28/12 TIME: 8:30 A.M. DEPT: B CASE NO: CV1204541

PRESIDING: HON. ROY O. CHERNUS

REPORTER: JO DILLINHAM BREWER, CSR 9707 CLERK: ~~DUONG THAI~~ S. DILLON

PLAINTIFF: BANK OF AMERICA, N.A.	EUGENE L. HAHN (π)
vs.	ROY HOPPE, Δ PRO PER KAYO KIMURA, Δ PRO PER
DEFENDANT: SAMUEL H. SLOAN, ET AL	FRANK THORNALLY, Δ PRO PER SAMUEL SLOAN, Δ PRO PER AND ADMINISTRATOR OF THE GOODALL TRUST

NATURE OF PROCEEDINGS: 1) MOTION FOR SUMMARY JUDGMENT – AGAINST SLOAN AND KIMURA [PLTF] BANK OF AMERICA, N.A.
2) MOTION FOR SUMMARY JUDGMENT – AGAINST DEFTS HOPPE AND THORNALLY [PLTF] BANK OF AMERICA, N.A.

ARGUED

RULING ADOPTED

Motions for Summary Judgment by Plaintiff Bank of America , N. A., Trustee of the Trust for Michael created under the Goodall Trust dated September 12, 1990, against defendants Samuel Sloan, Roy Hoppe, Frank Thornally, and Kayo Kimura are denied.

As against Sam Sloan and Kayo Kimura, plaintiff seeks judgment for possession based on orders of the San Francisco Superior Court and the July 27, 2012, Sixty-day notice. Plaintiff has put its title to the property "at issue" in this unlawful detainer proceeding. The bulk of the allegations in the Complaint and the "Undisputed Facts" in support of the subject motion for summary judgment are addressed to plaintiff's extensive efforts by way of collateral proceedings in San Francisco Superior Court to confirm that the premises is an asset of the Trust for Michael created under the Goodall Trust dated September 12, 1990, that title to the premises is in Bank of America as trustee, and that plaintiff may administer the premises pursuant to the terms of Trust. Yet despite plaintiff's extensive allegations detailing the San Francisco proceedings, plaintiff does not actually allege or demonstrate via undisputed facts that the orders of the SF Sup. Ct. are "final" or that the issue of its title to the subject property has been fully and finally determined. Plaintiff appears to base its right to commence this unlawful detainer proceeding upon the **Minute Order** of the SF Superior Court dated July 19, 2012, denying defendant's petition for reconsideration as plaintiff served the subject 60-Day Notice eight days later on July 27, 2012, ***even though the court's order was not formally entered until September 27, 2012.*** (See Complaint, ¶19, and Exh. E.) Even *assuming* the order denying defendant's petition for reconsideration constitutes a final and binding determination of plaintiff's title (though not specifically alleged), plaintiff served the 60-day notice before that Order was formally entered on September 27, 2012. This unlawful detainer action was filed a mere 12-days later on October 9,

2012. As stated by the Court in *Greenhut v. Wooden* (1982) 129 Cal.App.3d 64, 68, "this is not your usual garden variety type of unlawful detainer action" where the issue of title is strictly limited. Having put its own title in issue and by relying on the San Francisco Trust proceeding as the source of its authority to commence this proceeding, plaintiff should demonstrate that title to the property has, in fact, been finally adjudicated in its favor. Plaintiff's pleading and evidence falls short of demonstrating a final adjudication of title in its favor and raises a question of fact whether the alleged 60-day notice was served prematurely.

As to defendants Hoppe and Thornally, a complaint for unlawful detainer must allege that the tenant continues in possession of the premises. (CCP §1161.) No cause of action for unlawful detainer exists if the tenant has quit before the action is filed. Defendants Hoppe and Thornally have filed answers admitting they have relinquished possession of the premises. In its motion, plaintiff claims that while Hoppe and Thornally have relinquished physical possession of the premises, "plaintiff is informed that Hoppe and Thornally have not relinquished their alleged *right* to possession of the premises." If a landlord wishes to determine *rights* to possession, but not physical possession, it cannot do so by way of summary unlawful detainer; a quiet title action would be the proper remedy.

In the event that no party requests oral argument in accordance with Marin County Superior Court Local Rules, Rule 1.6 B., the prevailing party shall prepare an order consistent with the announced ruling as required by Marin County Superior Court Local Rules, Rule 1.7.

Superior Court of California, County of San Francisco
Case Number: PTR-99-273030
Title: IN RE: THE GOODALL TRUST
Cause of Action: TRUST
Generated: Feb-24-2013 2:25 pm PST

Register of Actions   Parties   Attorneys   Calendar   Payments   Documents

Register of Actions

Date Range: First Date Dec-21-1999   Last Date Feb-24-2013   (Dates must be entered as MMM-DD-YYYY)

Descending Date Sequence   ALL FILING TYPES   Submit

Date	Proceedings		
FEB-14-2013	CLERK'S ESTIMATE OF COST OF APPEAL RECORD-RESPONDENT	View	
FEB-07-2013	DESIGNATION OF THE RECORD ON APPEAL OF 11/26/12 ORDER FILED BY PETITIONER SLOAN, SAMUEL H	View	
FEB-07-2013	REQUEST FOR CLERK'S/REPORTER'S TRANSCRIPT FILED (RT ATTACHED TO DESIGNATION)	View	
JAN-28-2013	CLERK'S NOTICE OF FILING OF NOTICE OF APPEAL (FROM ORDER ENTERED 11-26-12)	View	
JAN-28-2013	CLERK'S NOTICE OF FILING OF NOTICE OF APPEAL (FROM ORDER ENTERED 11-15-12)	View	
JAN-28-2013	NOTICE OF APPEAL/REQUEST FOR TRANSCRIPT (NTC OF APPEAL ONLY) (APPEAL FROM ORDER ENTERED ON 11-26-13) FILED BY PLAINTIFF SLOAN, SAMUEL H	View	IFP
JAN-28-2013	NOTICE OF APPEAL/REQUEST FOR TRANSCRIPT (NTC OF APPEAL ONLY) (APPEAL FROM ORDER ENTERED 11-15-12) FILED BY PETITIONER SLOAN, SAMUEL H	View	IFP
JAN-16-2013	ORDER DISMISSING APPEAL (A137190 DIV 4)	View	
JAN-16-2013	ORDER DISMISSING APPEAL (A137189 DIV 4)	View	
JAN-11-2013	DESIGNATION OF RECORD OF SECOND APPEAL A137190 TO BE THE SAME AS THE RECORD OF FIRST APPEAL A137189	View	
DEC-26-2012	REQUEST FOR CLERK'S/REPORTER'S TRANSCRIPT FILED	View	
DEC-26-2012	APPLICATION FOR WAIVER OF COURT FEES AND COSTS PURSUANT TO G.C. 68633, CRC 3.51, 8.26, AND 8.818 (CONFIDENTIAL) FILED BY PLAINTIFF SLOAN, SAMUEL H ORDER FOR WAIVER OF COURT FEES AND COSTS GRANTED PURSUANT TO G.C. 68634 (E), CRC 3.52		
DEC-20-2012	ORDER GRANTING FEE WAIVER FOR COA A137189 AND A137190	View	
DEC-07-2012	NOTICE OF DEFAULT ON APPEAL SENT TO APPELLANT A137189 #4	View	
DEC-07-2012	NOTICE OF DEFAULT ON APPEAL SENT TO APPELLANT A137190 #4	View	
NOV-29-2012	CLERK'S NOTICE OF FILING OF NOTICE OF APPEAL (ORDER DATED 9/27/12)	View	
NOV-29-2012	CLERK'S NOTICE OF FILING OF NOTICE OF APPEAL (ORDER DATED 5/16/12)	View	
NOV-26-2012	ORDER DENYING MOTION FOR SANCTIONS	View	
NOV-21-2012	NOTICE OF APPEAL/REQUEST FOR TRANSCRIPT (NTC OF APPEAL ONLY) FILED BY PETITIONER SLOAN, SAMUEL H	View	100.00
NOV-21-2012	NOTICE OF APPEAL/REQUEST FOR TRANSCRIPT (NTC OF APPEAL ONLY) FILED BY PETITIONER SLOAN, SAMUEL H	View	100.00

NOV-15-2012	ORDER GRANTING ATTORNEY'S MOTION TO BE RELIEVED AS COUNSEL	View	
NOV-15-2012	TRUSTEE BANK OF AMERICA N.A.'S NOTICE OF MOTION AND MOTION FOR SANCTIONS PURSUANT TO CODE OF CIVIL PROCEDURE SECTIONS 128.7 AND 1008(D); MEMORANDUM OF POINTS AND AUTHORITIES IN SUPPORT THEREOF, CALENDAR OF NOV-15-2012, DENIED	View View	
NOV-15-2012	MOTION TO BE RELIEVED AS COUNSEL, CALENDAR OF OCT-29-2012, GRANTED PER WRITTEN ORDER	View	
NOV-15-2012	MINI MINUTES FOR NOV-15-2012 02:00 PM FOR DEPT 204	View	
NOV-14-2012	PROBATE OPPOSITION/OBJECTION TO TRUSTEE BANK OF AMERICA N.A.'S NOTICE OF MOTION AND MOTION FOR SANCTIONS PURSUANT TO CODE OF CIVIL PROCEDURE SECTIONS 128.7 AND 1008(D); MEMORANDUM OF POINTS AND AUTHORITIES IN SUPPORT THEREOF FILED BY OBJECTOR SLOAN, SAMUEL H	View View	
NOV-07-2012	DECLARATION SUPPLEMENTAL DECLARATION OF GARY D. ROTHSTEIN IN SUPPORT OF BANK OF AMERICA, N.A.'S MOTION FOR SANCTIONS AGAINST SAM SLOAN AND HIS COUNSEL PURSUANT TO CODE OF CIVIL PROCEDURE SECTIONS 128.7 AND 1008(D) FILED BY TRUSTEE BANK OF AMERICA NT & SA	View View	
NOV-07-2012	REPLY TRUSTEE BANK OF AMERICA, N.A.'S SUPPLEMENTAL REPLY IN SUPPORT OF MOTION FOR SANCTIONS PURSUANT TO CODE OF CIVIL PROCEDURE SECTIONS 128.7 AND 1008(D) FILED BY TRUSTEE BANK OF AMERICA NT & SA	View View	
NOV-01-2012	SUPPLEMENTAL OPPOSITION TO MOTION FOR SANCTIONS AND DECLARATION IN SUPPORT THEREOF FILED BY RESPONDENT WARE, SAM		
OCT-29-2012	MOTION TO BE RELIEVED AS COUNSEL, CALENDAR OF OCT-29-2012, GRANTED SUBJECT TO WRITTEN ORDER		
OCT-29-2012	MINI MINUTES FOR OCT-29-2012 10:30 AM FOR DEPT 204	View	
OCT 01 2012	NOTICE OF ENTRY OF ORDER/NOTICE OF RULING FILED FILED BY TRUSTEE BANK OF AMERICA NT & SA	View View	
SEP-27-2012	ORDER DENYING SAM SLOAN'S AMENDED NOTICE OF MOTION AND MOTION TO RECONSIDER (ERRONEOUSLY CAPTIONED EARLIER AS MOTION TO COMPEL PRODUCTION OF DOCUMENTS)	View View	
SEP-20-2012	TRUSTEE BANK OF AMERICA N.A.'S NOTICE OF MOTION AND MOTION FOR SANCTIONS PURSUANT TO CODE OF CIVIL PROCEDURE SECTIONS 128.7 AND 1008(D); MEMORANDUM OF POINTS AND AUTHORITIES IN SUPPORT THEREOF CONTINUED FROM SEP-20-2012 TO NOV-15-2012 AT 02:00 PM IN DEPT 204 PER COURT	View View	
SEP-20-2012	MOTION TO BE RELIEVED AS COUNSEL ADVANCED FROM OCT-30-2012 TO OCT-29-2012 AT 10:30 AM IN DEPT 204 PER COURT	View	
SEP-20-2012	MINI MINUTES FOR SEP-20-2012 02:30 PM FOR DEPT 204	View	
SEP-13-2012	TRUSTEE B OF A, N.A. REPLY IN SUPPORT IF MOTION FOR SANCTIONS PURSANT TO OOP SEC 128.7 AND 1008(D) FILED BY TRUSTEE BANK OF AMERICA NT & SA	View	
SEP-07-2012	DECLARATION IN SUPPORT OF ATTORNEY'S MOTION TO BE RELIEVED AS COUNSEL FILED BY PETITIONER SLOAN, SAMUEL H	View	
SEP-07-2012	MOTION TO BE RELIEVED AS COUNSEL FILED BY PETITIONER SLOAN, SAMUEL H HEARING SET FOR OCT-30-2012 AT 09:00 AM IN DEPT 204	View	60.00
SEP-07-2012	DECLARATION OF SAM WARE REGARDING SANCTIONS MOTION FILED BY PETITIONER SLOAN, SAMUEL H	View	
AUG-24-2012	PROBATE OPPOSITION/OBJECTION TO TRUSTEE BANK OF AMERICA N.A.'S NOTICE OF MOTION AND MOTION FOR SANCTIONS PURSUANT TO CODE OF CIVIL PROCEDURE SECTIONS 128.7 AND 1008(D); MEMORANDUM OF POINTS AND AUTHORITIES IN SUPPORT THEREOF FILED BY OBJECTOR SLOAN, SAMUEL H	View View	
AUG-14-2012	TRUSTEE BANK OF AMERICA N.A.'S NOTICE OF MOTION AND MOTION FOR SANCTIONS PURSUANT TO CODE OF CIVIL PROCEDURE SECTIONS 128.7 AND 1008(D); MEMORANDUM OF POINTS AND AUTHORITIES IN SUPPORT THEREOF CONTINUED FROM AUG-30-2012 TO SEP-20-2012 AT 02:30 PM IN DEPT 204 AT COUNSEL'S REQUEST PER COURT	View View	

AUG-10-2012	OPPOSITION TO MOTION FOR SANCTIONS AND DECLARATION IN SUPPORT THEREOF FILED BY PETITIONER SLOAN, SAMUEL H	View	
AUG-10-2012	STIPULATION TO CONTINUE HEARING OF MOTION FOR SANCTIONS FILED BY SLOAN, SAMUEL H	View	
JUL-23-2012	PROOF OF SERVICE BY MAIL FILED BY PETITIONER BANK OF AMERICA NT & SA	View	
JUL-20-2012	DECLARATION OF GARY D ROTHSTEIN IN SUPPORT OF BANK OF AMERICA, N.A.'S MOTION TO SANCTIONS AGAINST SAM SLOAN AND HIS COUNSEL PURSUANT TO CODE OF CIVIL PROCEDURE SECTIONS 128.7 AND 1008(D) FILED BY TRUSTEE BANK OF AMERICA NT & SA	View	
JUL-20-2012	TRUSTEE BANK OF AMERICA N.A.'S NOTICE OF MOTION AND MOTION FOR SANCTIONS PURSUANT TO CODE OF CIVIL PROCEDURE SECTIONS 128.7 AND 1008(D); MEMORANDUM OF POINTS AND AUTHORITIES IN SUPPORT THEREOF FILED BY TRUSTEE BANK OF AMERICA NT & SA HEARING SET FOR AUG-30-2012 AT 02:30 PM IN DEPT 204	View	60.00
JUL-19-2012	NOTICE OF MOTION AND MOTION TO COMPEL PRODUCTION OF DOCUMENTS AND FURTHER DEPOSITION AND DECLARATION OF SLOAN IN SUPPORT THEREOF, CALENDAR OF JUL-19-2012, DENIED		
JUL-19-2012	MINI MINUTES FOR JUL-19-2012 02:00 PM FOR DEPT 204		
JUL-12-2012	DECLARATION OF SAM WARE IN SUPPORT OF REPLY MEMORANDUM REGARDING MOTION TO RECONSIDER FILED BY PETITIONER SLOAN, SAMUEL H	View	
JUL-12-2012	REPLY MEMORANDUM REGARDING MOTION TO RECONSIDER FILED BY PETITIONER SLOAN, SAMUEL H	View	
JUL-06-2012	JOINDER IN BANK OF AMERICA, N.A.'S RESPONSE TO SAM SLOAN'S MOTION TO RECONSIDER FILED BY OBJECTOR GUIDE DOGS FOR THE BLIND	View	
JUL-02-2012	PROOF OF SERVICE BY MAIL FILED BY OBJECTOR BANK OF AMERICA NT & SA	View	
JUL-02-2012	DECLARATION OF GARY D. ROTHSTEIN IN SUPPORT OF BANK OF AMERICA, N.A.'S OPPOSITION TO SAM SLOAN'S AMENDED NOTICE OF MOTION AND MOTION FOR RECONSIDERATION FILED BY PETITIONER BANK OF AMERICA NT & SA	View	
JUL-02-2012	OPPOSITION BANK OF AMERICA, N.A.'S OPPOSITION TO SAM SLOAN'S AMENDED NOTICE OF MOTION AND MOTION TO RECEONSIDER [ERRONEOUSLY CAPTIONED EARLIER AS MOTION TO COMPLEL PRODUCTION OF DOCUMENTS] FILED BY OBJECTOR BANK OF AMERICA NT & SA	View	
JUN-29-2012	GUIDE DOGS FOR THE BLIND, INC.'S JOINDER IN TRUSTEE BANK OF AMERICA, N.A.'S MOTION FOR SANCTIONS PURSUANT TO CODE OF CIVIL PROCEDURE SECTIONS 128.7 AND 1008(D); MEMORANDUM OF POINTS AND AUTHORITIES IN SUPPORT THEREOF FILED BY OTHER GUIDE DOGS FOR THE BLIND	View	
JUN-19-2012	AMENDED NOTICE OF MOTION AND MOTION TO RECONSIDER [ERRONEOUSLY CAPTIONED EARLIER AS MOTION TO COMPEL PRODUCTION OF DOCUMENTS] FILED BY PETITIONER SLOAN, SAMUEL H	View	
JUN-05-2012	NOTICE OF MOTION AND MOTION TO COMPEL PRODUCTION OF DOCUMENTS AND FURTHER DEPOSITION AND DECLARATION OF SLOAN IN SUPPORT THEREOF CONTINUED FROM JUL-05-2012 TO JUL-19-2012 AT 02:00 PM IN DEPT 204 PER COURT		
MAY-25-2012	DECLARATION OF DAVID S. MOORE FILED BY PETITIONER SLOAN, SAMUEL H	View	
MAY-25-2012	NOTICE OF MOTION AND MOTION TO COMPEL PRODUCTION OF DOCUMENTS AND FURTHER DEPOSITION AND DECLARATION OF SLOAN IN SUPPORT THEREOF FILED BY PETITIONER SLOAN, SAMUEL H HEARING SET FOR JUL-05-2012 AT 02:00 PM IN DEPT 204	View	40.00
MAY-18-2012	NOTICE OF ENTRY OF ORDER/NOTICE OF RULING FILED FILED BY PETITIONER BANK OF AMERICA NT & SA	View	

MAY-16-2012	ORDER RESULTING FROM HEARING ON MAY 7, 2012: (1)DENYING THE AMENDED PETITION OF SAM SLOAN FOR FORENSIC DOCUMENT EXAMINATION OF DOCUMENTS PURPORTED TO BE TRUST DOCUMENTS OF THE GOODALL FAMILY TRUST; AND (2) GRANTING BANK OF AMERICA N.A.'S PETITION FOR DETERMINATION OF THE BENEFICIARIES TO WHOM TRUST PROPERTY SHALL PASS UPON TERMINATION OF TRUST	View	
MAY-15-2012	PETITION FOR DETERMINATION OF THE BENEFICIARIES TO WHOM TRUST PROPERTY SHALL PASS UPON TERMINATION OF TRUST, CALENDAR OF MAY-07-2012 - ORDER SIGNED		
MAY-10-2012	REPLY TO BANK OF AMERICA AND GUIDE DOGS OPPOSITION FILED LAST WEEK. FILED BY PETITIONER SLOAN, SAMUEL H	View	
MAY-07-2012	PETITION FOR DETERMINATION OF THE BENEFICIARIES TO WHOM TRUST PROPERTY SHALL PASS UPON TERMINATION OF TRUST, CALENDAR OF MAY-07-2012, GRANTED SUBJECT TO WRITTEN ORDER		
MAY-07-2012	PETITION FOR SAM SLAON FOR FORENSIC DOCUMETS EXAMINATION OF DOCUMENTS PURPORTED TO BE TRUST DOCUMENTS OF THE GOODALL FAMILY TRUST., CALENDAR OF MAY-07-2012, DENIED		
MAY-07-2012	MINI MINUTES FOR MAY-07-2012 09:00 AM FOR DEPT 204		
APR-24-2012	REPLY PETITIONER BANK OF AMERICA N.A.'S ADDITIONAL REPLY IN SUPPORT OF PETITION FOR DETERMINATION OF THE BENEFICARIES TO WHOM TRUST PROPERTYS SHALL BE PASS UPON TERMINATION OF TRUST.	View	
APR-24-2012	OPPOSITION TO SAM SLOANS FURTHER SUPPLEMENTAL OBJECTIONS TO PETITION FOR DETERMINATION OF BENEFICIARIES FILED BY OBJECTOR GUIDE DOGS FOR THE BLIND	View	
APR-10-2012	AMENDED PETITION OF SAM SLOAN FOR FORENSIC DOCUMENT EXAMINATION OF DOCUMENTS PURPORTED TO BE TRUST DOCUMENTS OF THE GOODALL FAMILY TRUST FILED BY PETITIONER SLOAN, SAMUEL H	View	
MAR-26-2012	NOTICE OF ENTRY OF ORDER/NOTICE OF RULING FILED FILED BY PETITIONER BANK OF AMERICA NT & SA	View	
MAR-20-2012	ORDER CONTINUING HEARING OF PETITION FOR DETERMINATION OF THE BENEFICIARIES TO WHOM TRUST PROPERTY SHALL PASS UPON TERMINATION OF TRUST; AND REQUIRING PAYMENT OF RENT	View	
MAR-07-2012	PETITION FOR DETERMINATION OF THE BENEFICIARIES TO WHOM TRUST PROPERTY SHALL PASS UPON TERMINATION OF TRUST CONTINUED FROM MAR-07-2012 TO MAY-07-2012 AT 09:00 AM IN DEPT 204 PER COURT		
MAR-07-2012	MINI MINUTES FOR MAR-07-2012 09:00 AM FOR DEPT 204		
MAR-02-2012	REPLY PETITIONER BANK OF AMERICA N.A.'S FURTHER REPLY IN SUPPORT OF PETITION FOR DETERMINATION OF THE BENEFICIARIES TO WHOM TRUST PROPERTY SHALL PASS UPON TERMINATION OF TRUST FILED BY PETITIONER BANK OF AMERICA NT & SA	View	
MAR-01-2012	PROOF OF SERVICE BY MAIL FILED BY PETITIONER SLOAN, SAMUEL H	View	
MAR-01-2012	PETITION FOR SAM SLAON FOR FORENSIC DOCUMETS EXAMINATION OF DOCUMENTS PURPORTED TO BE TRUST DOCUMENTS OF THE GOODALL FAMILY TRUST. FILED BY PETITIONER SLOAN, SAMUEL H HEARING SET FOR MAY-07-2012 AT 09:00 AM IN DEPT 204	View	410.00
MAR-01-2012	DECLARATION OF ALICIA ADORNATO IN SUPPORT OF GUIDE DOGS FOR THE BLIND, INC.'S OPPOSITION TO SAM SLOAN'S FURTHER SUPPLEMENTAL OBJECTIONS TO PETITION FOR DETERMINATION OF BENEFICIARIES FILED BY OBJECTOR GUIDE DOGS FOR THE BLIND	View	

MAR-01-2012	PROBATE OPPOSITION/OBJECTION TO PETITION FOR DETERMINATION OF THE BENEFICIARIES TO WHOM TRUST PROPERTY SHALL PASS UPON TERMINATION OF TRUST [OPPOSITION TO SAM SLOAN'S FURTHER SUPPLEMENTAL OBJECTIONS TO PETITION FOR DETERMINATION OF BENEFICIARIES] FILED BY OBJECTOR GUIDE DOGS FOR THE BLIND	View	410.00
FEB-28-2012	PETITION FOR DETERMINATION OF THE BENEFICIARIES TO WHOM TRUST PROPERTY SHALL PASS UPON TERMINATION OF TRUST CONTINUED FROM FEB-28-2012 TO MAR-07-2012 AT 09:00 AM IN DEPT 204 PER COURT		
FEB-14-2012	PETITION FOR DETERMINATION OF THE BENEFICIARIES TO WHOM TRUST PROPERTY SHALL PASS UPON TERMINATION OF TRUST CONTINUED FROM FEB-14-2012 TO FEB-28-2012 AT 09:00 AM IN DEPT 204 PER COURT		
FEB-08-2012	PETITION FOR DETERMINATION OF THE BENEFICIARIES TO WHOM TRUST PROPERTY SHALL PASS UPON TERMINATION OF TRUST CONTINUED FROM FEB-08-2012 TO FEB-14-2012 AT 09:00 AM IN DEPT 204 PER COURT		
FEB-06-2012	DECLARATION OF NANCY RODGERS FILED BY PETITIONER SLOAN, SAMUEL H	View	
FEB-06-2012	FURTHER SUPPLEMENTAL OBJECTIONS TO PETITION FOR DETERMINATION OF BENEFICIARIES FILED BY OBJECTOR SLOAN, SAMUEL H	View	
FEB-06-2012	OBJECTIONS TO EVIDENCE FILED BY OBJECTOR SLOAN, SAMUEL H	View	
FEB-06-2012	DECLARATION OF SAM SLOAN FILED BY OBJECTOR SLOAN, SAMUEL H	View	
FEB-02-2012	DECLARATION OF J. R HASTINGS PURSANT TO COURT ORDER ON RESPONDENT'S MOTION TO COMPEL PRODUCTION OF DOCUMENTS AND FURTHER DEPOSITION. FILED BY PETITIONER HASTINGS, JAMES	View	
JAN-20-2012	ORDER DENYING MOTION TO COMPEL PRODUCTION OF DOCUMENTS AND FUTHER DEPOSITION	View	
JAN-12-2012	NOTICE OF MOTION AND MOTION TO COMPEL PRODUCTION OF DOCUMENTS AND FURTHER DEPOSITION AND DECLARATION OF SAM WARE IN SUPPORT THEREOF AND MEMORANDUM OF POINTS AND AUTHORITIES, CALENDAR OF JAN-12-2012, DENIED		
JAN-12-2012	MINI MINUTES FOR JAN-12-2012 02:15 PM FOR DEPT 204		
JAN-05-2012	REPLY TO OPPOSITION TO MOTION FILED BY PETITIONER GOODALL, K. MICHAEL	View	
JAN-04-2012	GUIDE DOGS FOR THE BLIND, INC.'S JOINDER IN DEPONENT JAMES R. HASTINGS' OPPOSITION TO RESPOND TO SAM SLOAN'S MOTION TO COMPEL DOCUMENTS AND FURTHER DEPOSITION FILED BY OBJECTOR GUIDE DOGS FOR THE BLIND	View	
DEC-29-2011	DECLARATION OF DON A. LESSER OPPOSING RESPONDENT SAM SLOAN'S MOTION TO COMPEL PRODUCTION OF DOCUMENTS AND FURTHER DEPOSITION FILED BY PETITIONER HASTINGS, JAMES	View	
DEC-29-2011	PROOF OF SERVICE BY MAIL FILED BY PETITIONER HASTINGS, JAMES	View	
DEC-29-2011	PROBATE OPPOSITION/OBJECTION TO NOTICE OF MOTION AND MOTION TO COMPEL PRODUCTION OF DOCUMENTS AND FURTHER DEPOSITION AND DECLARATION OF SAM WARE IN SUPPORT THEREOF AND MEMORANDUM OF POINTS AND AUTHORITIES FILED BY OBJECTOR HASTINGS, JAMES	View	
DEC-21-2011	PETITION FOR DETERMINATION OF THE BENEFICIARIES TO WHOM TRUST PROPERTY SHALL PASS UPON TERMINATION OF TRUST CONTINUED FROM DEC-21-2011 TO FEB-08-2012 AT 09:00 AM IN DEPT 204 PER COURT		
DEC-14-2011	SEPARATE STATEMENT IN SUPPORT OF MOTION TO COMPEL PRODUCTION OF DOCUMENTS AND FURTHER DEPOSITION FILED BY PETITIONER SLOAN, SAMUEL H	View	
DEC-14-2011	NOTICE OF MOTION AND MOTION TO COMPEL PRODUCTION OF DOCUMENTS AND FURTHER DEPOSITION AND DECLARATION OF SAM WARE IN SUPPORT THEREOF AND MEMORANDUM OF POINTS AND AUTHORITIES FILED BY PETITIONER GOODALL, K. MICHAEL HEARING SET FOR JAN-12-2012 AT 02:15 PM IN DEPT 204	View	40.00
NOV-15-2011	PETITION FOR DETERMINATION OF THE BENEFICIARIES TO WHOM TRUST PROPERTY SHALL PASS UPON TERMINATION OF TRUST CONTINUED FROM NOV-15-2011 TO DEC-21-2011 AT 09:00 AM IN DEPT 204 PER COURT		

NOV-10-2011	SUBSTITUTION OF ATTORNEY: WARE, SAMUEL GILMORE SUBSTITUTED FOR PRO PER AS ATTORNEY FOR SLOAN, SAMUEL H	View	
AUG-23-2011	PETITION FOR DETERMINATION OF THE BENEFICIARIES TO WHOM TRUST PROPERTY SHALL PASS UPON TERMINATION OF TRUST CONTINUED FROM AUG-23-2011 TO NOV-15-2011 AT 09:00 AM IN DEPT 204 PER COURT		
AUG-23-2011	MINI-MINUTES FOR AUG-23-2011 9:00 AM FOR DEPT 204		
AUG-19-2011	PETITIONER'S BANK OF AMERICA, N.A.'S REPLY IN SUPPORT OF PETN. TO DETERMINATION OF THE BENEFICIARIES TO WHOM TRUST PROPERTY SHALL PASS UPON TERMINATION OF TRUST FILED BY TRUSTEE BANK OF AMERICA NT & SA	View	
AUG-19-2011	DECLARATION OF J.R. HASTINGS FAMILY AND ESTATE PLANNING ATTORNEY FOR THE GOODALLS FILED BY PETITIONER HOPPE, ROY THORNALLY, FRANK	View	
AUG-12-2011	SUPPLEMENTAL OBJECTIONS TO POETITION FGOT DETERMINATION OF BENEFICIARIES AND REQUEST FOR CONTINUANCE OF HEARING. FILED BY PETITIONER GOODALL, K. MICHAEL	View	
JUL-29-2011	FURTHER PROBATE OPPOSITION/OBJECTION TO PETITION FOR DETERMINATION OF THE BENEFICIARIES TO WHOM TRUST PROPERTY SHALL PASS UPON TERMINATION OF TRUST FILED BY OBJECTOR SAMUEL H. SLOAN FILED BY OBJECTOR SLOAN, SAMUEL H	View	
JUL-25-2011	PROOF OF SERVICE BY MAIL FILED BY TRUSTEE BANK OF AMERICA NT & SA	View	
JUL-11-2011	PETITION FOR DETERMINATION OF THE BENEFICIARIES TO WHOM TRUST PROPERTY SHALL PASS UPON TERMINATION OF TRUST CONTINUED FROM JUL-11-2011 TO AUG-23-2011 AT 09:00 AM IN DEPT 204 PER COURT		
JUL-11-2011	MINI-MINUTES FOR JUL-11-2011 9:00 AM FOR DEPT 204		
JUL-05-2011	PROBATE OPPOSITION/OBJECTION TO PETITION FOR DETERMINATION OF THE BENEFICIARIES TO WHOM TRUST PROPERTY SHALL PASS UPON TERMINATION OF TRUST FILED BY OBJECTOR SLOAN, SAMUEL H	View	410.00
JUN-10-2011	PROOF OF SERVICE BY MAIL FILED BY TRUSTEE BANK OF AMERICA NT & SA	View	
JUN-10-2011	COPYING FEES (3 PAGE, 1 CERTIFIED COPY)		26.50
JUN-08-2011	NOTICE OF HEARING FILED BY TRUSTEE BANK OF AMERICA NT & SA	View	
JUN-08-2011	PETITION FOR DETERMINATION OF THE BENEFICIARIES TO WHOM TRUST PROPERTY SHALL PASS UPON TERMINATION OF TRUST FILED BY TRUSTEE BANK OF AMERICA NT & SA HEARING SET FOR JUL-11-2011 AT 09:00 AM IN DEPT 204	View	410.00
JUN-03-2011	ORDER CONFIRMING REAL PROPERTY AS AN ASSET OF THE TRUST	View	
JUN-03-2011	PETITION FOR ORDER CONFIRMING REAL RPOPERTY AS AN ASSET OF THE TRUST, CALENDAR OF MAY-25-2011, GRANTED PER WRITTEN ORDER		
MAY-25-2011	PETITION FOR ORDER CONFIRMING REAL RPOPERTY AS AN ASSET OF THE TRUST, CALENDAR OF MAY-25-2011, TAKEN UNDER SUBMISSION AS OF MAY-25-2011		
MAY-25-2011	MINI-MINUTES FOR MAY-25-2011 9:00 AM FOR DEPT 204		
MAY-20-2011	PROBATE OPPOSITION/OBJECTION TO PETITION FOR ORDER CONFIRMING REAL RPOPERTY AS AN ASSET OF THE TRUST FILED BY OBJECTOR SLOAN, SAMUEL H	View	410.00
APR-25-2011	PROOF OF SERVICE BY MAIL & PERSONAL SERVICE FILED BY TRUSTEE BANK OF AMERICA NT & SA	View	
APR-21-2011	NOTICE OF HEARING FILED BY TRUSTEE BANK OF AMERICA NT & SA	View	
APR-21-2011	PETITION FOR ORDER CONFIRMING REAL RPOPERTY AS AN ASSET OF THE TRUST FILED BY TRUSTEE BANK OF AMERICA NT & SA HEARING SET FOR MAY-25-2011 AT 09:00 AM IN DEPT 204	View	410.00
MAR-28-2000	PETITION FOR REMOVAL OF TRUSTEE, CALENDAR OF MAR-27-2000, DENIED WITHOUT PREJUDICE		
MAR-28-2000	CALENDAR MOTION: REMOVAL OF TRUSTEE, CALENDAR OF MAR-27-2000, OFF CALENDAR DUPLICATE ENTRY. PER COURT		

MAR-21-2000	DECLARATION OF JAMES R. HASTINGS		
MAR-21-2000	PROOF OF SERVICE		
MAR-21-2000	MEMORANDUM OF POINTS AND AUTHORITIES IN OPPOSITION TO MOTION		
MAR-21-2000	DECLARATION OF SUSAN SCRIBNER		
MAR-21-2000	MEMORANDUM OF POINTS AND AUTHORITIES IN OPPOSITION TO MOTION		
MAR-21-2000	DECLARATION OF SUSAN SCRIBNER		
MAR-21-2000	MEMORANDUM OF POINTS AND AUTHORITIES IN SUPPORT OF MOTION		
FEB-16-2000	CONSENT TO ACT AS SUCCESSOR-TRUSTEE		
FEB-14-2000	PROOF OF SERVICE BY MAIL FILED		
FEB-14-2000	PETITION FOR REMOVAL OF TRUSTEE HEARING SET FOR MAR-27-2000 AT 09:30 AM IN DEPT 204		
FEB-14-2000	CALENDAR MOTION: REMOVAL OF TRUSTEE HEARING SET FOR MAR-27-2000 AT 09:30 AM IN DEPT 204		
FEB-09-2000	ORDER RE: PETN. RE: DETERMINATION THAT PARTICULAR ACTION BY BENEF. DOES NOT CONSTITUTE A CONSENT MICROFILMED R/B F: 319/ 20		
FEB-02-2000	MEMORANDUM OF POINTS AND AUTHORITIES IN OPPOSITION TO PET. RE DETERMINATION OF THE PARTICULAR ACTION BY BENEFICIARY		
FEB-02-2000	DECLARATION OF SUSAN D. SCRIBNER		
JAN-11-2000	CONSENT TO ACT AS SUCCESSOR-TRUSTEE		
DEC-21-1999	PETITION RE DETERMINATION THAT PARTICULAR ACTION BY BENEFICIARY DOES NOT CONSTITUTE A CONTEST HEARING SET FOR FEB-09-2000 AT 09:30 AM IN DEPT 204		
DEC-21-1999	PROOF OF SERVICE BY MAIL FILED		
DEC-21-1999	CALENDAR MOTION: OTHER HEARING SET FOR FEB-09-2000 AT 09:30 AM IN DEPT 204		
DEC-21-1999	$196.00 PD BY: K. MICHAEL GOODALL		

Printed in Dunstable, United Kingdom

91222422R00040